Climbing Everest

TALES OF TRIUMPH AND TRAGEDY ON
THE WORLD'S HIGHEST MOUNTAIN

BY AUDREY SALKELD

NATIONAL GEOGRAPHIC

WASHINGTON, D.C.

For all Everesters, past, present, and in the future. — AS

The author gratefully acknowledges the assistance of Roger Bilham.

The body text of the book is set in Stone Serif. The display text is set in Badhouse Bold.

Library of Congress Cataloging–in–Publication Data
Salkeld, Audrey
   Climbing Everest: tales of triumph and tragedy on the world's highest mountain / by Audrey Salkeld.
     p. cm.
   Includes bibliographical references and index.
   Contents: Because it's there: George Mallory attempts the climb — On top of the world: Tenzing Norgay reaches the top — Red flag in the summit snow: Chinese expedition finds new ways — Everest by "fair means": Reinhold Messner marches to his own drumbeat —Kangshung Face: the east side story: American team tries the other side — Everest for everyone? Rob Hall and Scott Fischer's groups face deadly storm.
  ISBN 0-7922-5105-9 (hard)
  1. Mountaineering—Everest, Mount (China and Nepal)—History—Juvenile literature.
2. Everest, Mount (China and Nepal)—Description and travel—Juvenile literature.
[1. Mountaineering. 2. Everest, Mount (China and Nepal)] I. Title.

GV199.44.E85 S22 2003
796.52'2'095496—dc21   2002032142

Published by the National Geographic Society

John M. Fahey, Jr., President and Chief Executive Officer
Gilbert M. Grosvenor, Chairman of the Board
Nina D. Hoffman, Executive Vice President, President of Books and School Publishing

Staff for This Book

Nancy Laties Feresten, Vice President, Editor–in–Chief of Children's Books

Bea Jackson, Art Director, Children's Books

Jennifer Emmett, Project Editor

Marty Ittner, Designer

Barbara Sheppard, Illustrations Editor

Janet Dustin, Illustrations Coordinator

Carl Mehler, Director of Maps

Joseph F. Ochlak, Map Research

Matt Chwastyk, Map Production

Jim Enzinna, Indexing

R. Gary Colbert, Production Director

Lewis R. Bassford, Production Manager

Vincent P. Ryan, Manufacturing Manager

TITLE PAGE: In a wild tangle of peaks, the summit of Everest can be seen rearing above the mighty Nuptse-Lhotse wall. This image repeats on each chapter opener page.

Author's Note

After having been fascinated by Everest since childhood, I'd almost given up hope of seeing the Himalaya for myself when, at the grand old age of fifty, I was invited to join a team going to look for clues to what happened to Mallory and Irvine. I would be "Expedition historian." I don't think there ever had been such a creature before and I didn't expect there to be again (although in that I was mistaken.) We didn't solve the 1924 mystery that year, but Everest exceeded my expectations. It is so beautiful, viewed from the North.

Base Camp in Tibet lies at almost 17,000 feet, where there is less than half the amount of oxygen in the air as at sea-level. It takes getting used to. At first you fight for breath, and every movement becomes an effort. Even in bed you think hard before rolling over as it exhausts you so much. You don't sleep well, though when you do you dream amazingly. I was lucky not to suffer the headaches and sickness some endure, but it still took a week or two to acclimatize sufficiently to move around comfortably at that level. In time, I was able to follow the climbers up the East Rongbuk Valley to Advance Base at 21,300 feet below the North Col. I stayed there a few days, but never felt lively enough to explore higher.

Ten years later, in 1996, I was lucky to visit Everest again, this time going to the Nepalese side with David Breashears's Imax filming team. Base Camp on this side is somewhat higher and pitched, not on bare ground, but on the rubble-covered ice of the Khumbu Glacier, at the foot of the stupendous Khumbu Icefall. Here, on the afternoon of May 10, I saw boiling dark clouds roll up the valley. A fierce storm was blowing in. With incredulous dismay and a sense of impotence, I watched events unfolding over the next couple of days that cost the lives of 8 climbers on the mountain. I saw Colonel Madan's little helicopter, no more than a bright dot seen from Base Camp, dip twice into the Western Cwm to rescue frost-bitten survivors Makalu Gau and Beck Weathers.

I may never get to Everest again, but I have to confess to an abiding longing to see its third massive flank as well, the great Kangshung Face. Who knows?

AUDREY SALKELD
Cumbria, 2002

PETER BOARDMAN AND JOE TASKER climbing Everest's Northeast Ridge in 1982 before they disappeared higher on the mountain. Beyond is Chomo Lonzo, below the Kangshung Glacier, and on the horizon Kangchenjunga.

Table of Contents

GEORGE MALLORY, ice ax in hand, makes it his first task on reaching
Everest in 1921 to train porters in ice-climbing techniques.

Introduction

The summit of Mount Everest, at 29,035 feet, reaches higher above sea level than anywhere else on the face of this planet. Geographically, Everest lies in the Khumbu Himal, one of the regions of the Greater Himalaya. Politically, the mountain straddles the border between Tibet and Nepal.

Everest is a massive pyramid with three dramatic ridges that define three steep mountainfaces. Two of these faces, the North and the East, fall within Tibet. The third, the Southwest Face, with its Khumbu Icefall and Glacier, overlooks Nepal.

Mount Everest was discovered to be the highest mountain in the world in the middle of the 19th century when the first detailed maps of India were being made by British cartographers as part of the Survey of India. At that time, outsiders were banned from entering Tibet or Nepal, so surveyors had to take their readings of Everest and its neighboring peaks from a great distance away. The data was supplemented with information gathered by native observers who were sent as spies into these forbidden countries. When all the information was brought together and processed, it became obvious that the mountain known then simply as "Peak 15" was a real monster. The story goes that one day in 1852 the Bengali chief computer—computers were men in those days, not machines—burst into his boss's office shouting, "Sir! Sir! I've found the highest mountain in the world!"

His calculations had produced a height of 29,002 feet for the peak, putting it well above Kangchenjunga, which till then had been thought to be the world's highest. Over the years, as surveyors were able to obtain other readings from closer to the mountain, the height was adjusted slightly upward. Nowadays, satellite and laser technology have pinned it at its present 29,035 feet—a figure quite close to the original calculations made by the painstaking pioneers of the Indian survey.

It was obvious that such an important mountain needed a name; a mere number simply wouldn't do. "Mount Everest" was suggested as a way of honoring Sir George Everest, who had inspired and supervised the Survey of India, and this was formally adopted by geographers in 1865. It remains the name by which most people recognize the mountain today, but what those old surveyors hadn't fully appreciated was that there already existed a well-established local name. Tibetans and Sherpas on either side of the international boundary that cuts through the mountain knew it as "Chomolungma"—which is usually translated as "Mother Goddess of the Land."

Not long after Everest (or Chomolungma) was confirmed as the pinnacle of the world people began wondering about the possibility of climbing it. Could humans survive on a summit as high as that? It was well known that as you climb higher, there is less oxygen available to breathe. Three French scientists flew a balloon to the same height as Everest in 1875. Rising rapidly, they all passed out—two never to wake again. Would the same thing happen if you ascended that high on foot, even though you would be rising more slowly? No one knew the answer to that, and it would be a long time before anyone could put the question to the test.

Once the North and South Poles had been reached in the early years of the 20th century, the lofty summit of Everest—often called the Third Pole—was seen as the greatest physical challenge left to adventurous spirits. Beginning in 1921 when climbers first obtained permission to approach Everest through Tibet, several British expeditions set out in the hope of being first to reach the roof of the world.

After decades of effort, Everest was first summitted in 1953 by Edmund Hillary and Tenzing Norgay, who carried extra oxygen to help them breathe in the thin air. After that, mountaineers believed people would lose interest in the great mountain, but that has not happened. Men and women from all around the world were inspired by the achievement. They saw film of the climb, read the many books and articles written about it, and tried to imagine what it would be like to stand up there in the unearthly territory of the summit. Then they began arriving to have a crack at it themselves. Their numbers have gone on increasing over the half century since that first ascent. Today, well over a thousand people have stood on the airy pinnacle: men, women, boys as young as 16, oldies in their late 60s. Some people have been up several times; one Sherpa has just announced his retirement after making 12 ascents. This book tells just a few stories from this rich history—signposts along the way. They're meant to convey a sense of the struggle involved in climbing the world's highest peak and portray the remarkable men and women who take on the quest.

Although its difficulties are better understood now and equipment is much better, Everest remains a dangerous place. More than 170 people have died on its slopes. Few years pass without fatalities. Yet its attraction does not diminish. Always, there are adventurous souls who want to know if, just for a fraction of time, they too can enjoy the sensation of being the highest person in the whole wide world.

MASSES OF LINE laid out to avoid tangles as climbers attempt to rig an ambitious if controversial tramway for ferrying loads up the steep initial buttress on Everest's East Face.

GEORGE MALLORY
UNITED KINGDOM

1886–1924

Explored and climbed on Everest
with expeditions in 1921, 1922, and 1924

Summit ascents: unknown

Because It's There!

The first mountaineers who set out to climb Everest had no clear idea of what to expect. They didn't even fully know what the mountain looked like, or how to reach it. Tucked away in the secret lands of Tibet and Nepal, it had been visible only from a distance.

For decades mountaineers had sought permission to travel inside these countries, but it wasn't until the 1920s that the Dalai Lama, Tibet's leader, gave his reluctant consent for a British party to approach Mount Everest through Tibet. He agreed the group could attempt a climb of the mountain, although as Buddhists, Tibetans were uneasy about anyone going up the high mountains. For them, these were holy places. Once the precious "passport" was received, the first explorers left England for the Himalaya. With no detailed maps of the area, their initial task was to tramp around Everest as far as possible, taking photographs and mapping its glaciers and ridges. If, as was hoped, a promising-looking way to the summit presented itself, a climbing team would return the following year.

THE EXPEDITION SET out from Darjeeling, India for the long trek over the mountains into Tibet in the middle of May 1921. Its members included a couple of surveyors, a geologist, a naturalist, two seasoned Himalayan travelers, and three mountaineers. They were accompanied by many Sherpa and Tibetan porters, cooks, and baggage mules. The strongest climber was 33-year-old George Mallory, an adventurous English schoolmaster, who is remembered today as the spirit of the enterprise. George Mallory is the man who, when asked why anyone should want to climb Mount Everest, reputedly replied, "Because it's there!"

From the steamy forests and tea gardens of Sikkim, the party crossed to the barren tableland of Tibet with its strong, chill winds. Suddenly, just visible on the horizon, a hundred miles in the distance, was the mountain they had come so far to see. Spirits lifted and Mallory wrote home to his wife, Ruth, "We're just about to walk off the map....It's beginning to be exciting."

Traveling in a great arc, they approached Everest from the north, and toward the end of June established their first camp in the shadow of the great mountain. At once Mallory set to giving the porters some necessary lessons in ice climbing. Then, for three months, he and the others defied bad weather as they explored to the north and east of Everest. They couldn't go around to the southern slopes because these lay inside Nepal.

Tirelessly, they tramped glaciers, climbed lesser peaks as viewpoints, and scrambled over passes. In the last days of the expedition Mallory led his friend Guy Bullock, map-maker Oliver Wheeler, and the three strongest porters from a windy camp under the rim of the

Lhakpa La Pass and across the snow basin at the head of the East Rongbuk Glacier. Ahead, the steep, snow-laden slopes of the North Col rose to 23,000 feet. This col, or saddle formation, links Everest's North Ridge with the neighboring peak of Changtse.

By 11:30 a.m., the group struggled to the top of the col, where a gale was blowing. Mallory wrote that the devil was dancing up there in a whirlwind of snow that took his breath away. Above them, more blown snow blurred the view of the rising ridge, but so far as Mallory could make out, no special difficulties lurked up there. He felt certain that with fresher men and less wind, this route could lead them to the summit; but it would be madness to go higher now with exhausted men. The party turned back.

It was too late in the season to try again. To Ruth, Mallory wrote, "It is a disappointment, there is no getting over it, that the end should be so much tamer than I hoped." Yet, he was sure no man could have survived for more than an hour up there in that wind. "As it is," he continued, "we have established the way to the summit for anyone who cares to try the highest adventure."

Within a few months Mallory was back, as a member of a larger party, with more experienced mountaineers in the team. Gen. Charlie Bruce was leader, and among the newcomers were Maj. Edward Norton, Dr. Howard Somervell, and George Ingle Finch. Henry Morshead, who had been one of the surveyors in 1921, came again, but as a climber this time; and a young cousin of the general's, Geoffrey Bruce, was hired to help organize the porters and baggage animals. He proved himself also as a stouthearted climber. It was a happy, friendly party, and at first the progress was good. A chain of

CLIMBING THE NORTH RIDGE during the 1922 expedition. Somervell took this photograph of his companions Mallory (left) and Norton approaching their record-setting high point of 26,985 feet. They were climbing without oxygen tanks.

camps was set up along the East Rongbuk Glacier, and more tents were pitched on top of the North Col. Once members became accustomed to that altitude, two more tents were erected in the lee of the North Ridge at a height of 24,000 feet to become Camp 5.

From here, after a sleepless, headachy night, Mallory, Norton, and Somervell set out toward the summit. They were climbing without oxygen apparatus and the going was painfully slow as they fought for breath in the thin air. By early afternoon, it became clear they would not reach the Northeast Shoulder that day—the place where the North Ridge joins the Northeast Ridge leading to the summit. Disappointed, they turned back. Collecting Morshead, who had been too ill that morning to accompany them, they made their way back to the North Col, roped together. At one point, on steep ground, Morshead slipped, pulling Norton and Somervell with him, but Mallory's quick reaction saved them all. Ramming in his ice ax, he quickly belayed himself and with supreme strength was able to hold the rope and halt the falling men. Badly shaken, they reached the North Col camp after dark. No one was there, nor were there any cooking stoves to melt snow to drink. They stirred canned milk, jam, and snow together to quench their raging thirst. They knew they had been lucky to survive.

A few days later Finch and Geoffrey Bruce had a go. They used extra oxygen that enabled them to move more easily, but the apparatus was heavy and awkward. Whenever they stopped to change to a new oxygen cylinder, they'd send the empty one clanging down the mountain with a gleeful, "Another five pounds off our backs!"

They struck out across the slabs of the North Face, moving unroped for speed. The summit crept closer as they gained both height and horizontal distance. Then Bruce let out a startled cry. His oxygen had ceased flowing, and the sudden sensation of breathing only thin air caused him to stumble drunkenly. Finch was able to make a temporary repair, but he could see that, tired as they were, one or both of them risked never coming back if they pressed on. He hated giving up, but they had set a new climbing record of 27,500 feet, and he supposed he should be proud of that.

By this time, most of the team were exhausted. Mallory, however, was unwilling to accept defeat. He thought they should push themselves for one last try, even though the flanks of the North Col were plastered in new snow. As the climbers were leading 14 porters up these slopes again, an avalanche caught the party, carrying away the men at the end of the line. These unfortunates were swept over an ice cliff and into a crevasse to be buried under masses of tumbled ice and snow. Seven porters died, and Mallory was devastated. He held himself responsible for the catastrophe.

When the next expedition was organized in Spring 1924, Mallory was of two minds about going. He hated the prospect of leaving his family, yet he could not reconcile himself to others climbing the mountain without him. Telling friends it would be more like war than adventure this time and that he'd be lucky to return alive, he set off again. It was his duty, he felt, to finish what he'd started. Mallory was the only climber to take part in all three Everest expeditions of the 1920s.

Mount Everest
29,035 ft
8,850 m

Oxygen bottle
found here, 1991
27,760 ft

Second
Step
28,280 ft

First
Step
28,110 ft

Irvine's ice axe
found near
here, 1933
27,700 ft

Northeast Ridge

Somervell's
highpoint
28,000 ft

Norton's
highpoint
28,126 ft

West Ridge

Great (Norton) Couloir

North Face

Camp 6
26,800 ft

North Ridge

Odell's position at
sighting, June 8, 1924
26,000 ft

Mallory found
here, 1999
26,760 ft

Changtse
(Bei Peak)

Camp 5
25,300 ft

CHINA

TIBET
Lhasa

PAKISTAN

NEPAL

HIMALAYA

BHUTAN

Kathmandu

Darjeeling

MT. EVEREST

INDIA

Arabian
Sea

Bay of
Bengal

0   miles   600

0   kilometers   900

1924 Expedition

—— Mallory and Irvine route

- - - Intended route to the summit

—— Somervell and Norton route

EVEREST'S NORTH FACE: The
climbers of 1924 were divided over the best
way to approach the summit. Norton favored
crossing the upper face toward the Great
Couloir; Mallory thought it preferable to follow
the Northeast Ridge. We suppose that is the
way he went with Irvine on his last climb, but
neither man returned to tell the tale. It was
75 years before Mallory's fallen body was
found. It is unclear where Irvine lies.

THE LAST PHOTOGRAPH OF MALLORY AND IRVINE ALIVE
was taken by team member Noel Odell. It shows them preparing to leave their camp
on the North Col on June 6. They died two days later.

"It's fifty to one against us but we'll have a whack yet and do ourselves proud."

—GEORGE MALLORY

This time General Bruce brought eight mountaineers, fit and in their prime. Norton and Somervell were there again, along with newcomers John de Vars Hazard, Noel Odell, and a university student, Andrew Irvine. Known to everyone as "Sandy," Irvine was studying to be an engineer. He was only 21 at the start of the expedition.

Mallory and Irvine got along from the minute they met on the boat. By the time they reached Everest on April 29, they were already working as a team and anxious to get climbing. Unfortunately, the expedition was greeted by a biting wind and snow, and it would have been better to wait before pitching camps and ferrying loads up the East Rongbuk Glacier. Instead, Mallory and Irvine led a protesting band of porters through blizzards to the site of Camp 3 under the North Col. As they climbed, everyone suffered badly from the unaccustomed altitude, only to find, when they got there, that not enough food, stoves, or bedding had been carried up. A viciously cold night at 21,300 feet left many porters sick and vomiting by morning. Some developed terrible frostbite. Mallory raced up and down between the glacier camps trying to get men and loads in the right places, but it was no good. The whole dispirited team was forced to retreat to base.

Time was ticking by. The North Col had not been reached, yet everyone was exhausted already. Worst of all, two of the staff died, one from frostbite and another from a suspected blood clot on the brain brought about by high altitude.

The team's second attempt to get higher also met with a setback. This time some porters became cut off on the North Col in a fierce snowstorm. They had to be rescued in just the unstable avalanche conditions that the team had been trying to avoid.

THE SNOW-HEAVY SLOPES OF THE NORTH COL: The photographer looked anxiously upward from Camp 3 as Mallory, Somervell, and Crawford led a column of climbers. Minutes later, the scene was blotted out. An avalanche had swept away many of the men. When the snow settled some figures could be seen struggling free, but seven porters had died, swallowed by a crevasse.

Norton, who had taken over leadership when General Bruce became sick, called a council of war. He wanted to forget about ferrying up oxygen bottles—effort that tied up so many of the porters. Instead, he proposed two pairs of climbers make separate dashes for the summit without oxygen if conditions allowed. Mallory thought this was madness. He'd been slow to appreciate the benefit of using bottled oxygen, but after Finch and Geoffrey Bruce climbed higher in 1922 using it, he was converted. He had no interest in merely gaining a few feet more of altitude. The climb needed to be done this time. It made no sense to keep coming back year after year. To Mallory's mind, dispensing with oxygen was throwing away any chance of success. But he had to abide by Norton's decision.

Accordingly, two dashes were made. First, Mallory and Geoffrey Bruce moved up the North Ridge to set up Camp 5, but were unable to coax their tired porters any further. Then, Somervell and Norton moved up and successfully placed a higher tent (Camp 6) in a little rocky basin at 26,800 feet on the North Face, where they passed a fitful night. Next morning they got up early and cautiously picked their way across tilted, gravel-coated slabs until they reached a distinctive band of yellow limestone encircling the mountain. The altitude was taking a toll. Every few yards the men drooped over their ice axes, gasping for breath.

At 28,000 feet, Somervell could go no farther, so Norton pressed on alone toward the gash in the North Face that is now known as Norton's Couloir. Climbing this, he said, would be like climbing the steep tiles of a roof. It was too dangerous for a single, unroped climber. Although the summit pyramid looked tantalizingly close, he turned back from a point later calculated as 28,126 feet.

Meanwhile, Mallory was restless. Storm-laden monsoon winds—which would put a stop to all climbing—had not yet arrived; again, he felt it was too soon to give up. If Norton and Somervell failed, as he expected, then he and Irvine should have one last "whack," using oxygen. Irvine was all for the idea. The two dashed down to base and back, gathering stores, oxygen bottles, and fit porters.

Early on Friday, June 6, with Norton's blessing, Mallory and Irvine set off from the North Col camp, accompanied by porters carrying all the available oxygen cylinders. That night they slept at Camp 5, and the next at 6. All the porters returned safely.

What happened on June 8, nobody knows for certain.

Odell followed up the mountain a day behind Mallory and Irvine. On the morning of the 8th, as he made his way up, banks of clouds began sweeping in from the west, impeding his view. Toward 1 p.m. the mists rolled back a little and Odell saw two tiny dots silhouetted high on the ridge above him. It had to be Mallory and Irvine. He was sure he was not mistaken: It was two moving men, heading toward the summit. Before the mists hid them from view, one appeared to have climbed up and joined the other on the second of two prominent rock steps on the ridge, the so-called Second Step. Unfortunately, in the years that followed, Odell wavered over exactly where he saw this vision. Successive generations of climbers have argued over what landmarks best fit his description, and indeed over whether he'd seen anything at all.

Mallory and Irvine did not come back. To this day no one knows whether they reached the top of Mount Everest before they vanished into legend. Mallory always said he wanted to follow the crest of the

THE BLANKET SIGNAL laid out in the snow on the North Col to advise those below that Mallory and Irvine had been given up for dead.

"All of a sudden, a patch of white, different from the snow and bright as marble, caught my eye."

—CONRAD ANKER

Northeast Ridge to the summit—and if we believe Odell's testimony—he would seem to have been attempting that. Yet we cannot be quite sure which way the two went.

At intervals over time later climbers would find the odd clue: an ice ax, an oxygen cylinder. In the 1970s, a Chinese climber was rumored to have reported seeing an old English body around 26,600 feet, but he took no pictures. Then, in 1999, 75 years after Mallory and Irvine disappeared, American climbers made an astonishing discovery. They were members of an expedition that included climber Conrad Anker, and they were specifically looking for evidence to what happened in 1924.

The expedition fanned out across and around the area where the Chinese climber had reported seeing an old English body. Something marble-white caught Conrad Anker's eye, and as he drew closer, he saw that the bright patch was a man. He saw bleached skin, a hobnailed boot, a section of old-fashioned climbing rope. The man, well preserved and looking like a fallen statue, was lying face down on the slope, his head uphill, and both arms outstretched. When Anker's companions joined him, they realized they had found George Mallory.

Items found in Mallory's pack and pockets—goggles, altimeter, oxygen calculations, etc.—gave poignant clues to that day in June 1924 when the most famous climber of his age set out to climb the world's highest mountain with his young companion. Nothing, however, survived to suggest how high the two men had climbed, or if they had reached the top. It may be that one day someone will come across an undamaged camera containing exposed film. Perhaps then, precious images may tell us more, but nothing can ever reveal what caused Mallory's and Irvine's fatal fall.

Everest Geography

The Himalaya are among the youngest mountains on Earth. They were formed as the result of a collision between two tectonic plates. The crust of the Earth is made up of a jigsaw puzzle of these plates, which carry the various continents. Sometimes they collide with each other; sometimes they spread apart. The mass that today is India tore away from a southern supercontinent we call Gondwana, some 135 million years ago, and drifted north, as a large island, toward the Asian continent. When it eventually scrunched into Asia, many million years later, its leading edge slid underneath Tibet and in the process caused a great crumpling of the Earth's surface. The Himalayan ranges were thrust up, forming the largest and highest upland on Earth above sea level. And the process continues. India still rams relentlessly into Asia, and the Himalaya continue to rise. Geophysicists say that Everest (29,035 feet) is growing by about a quarter of an inch each year.

All the while the mountains are slowly rising, strong forces are wearing them down again. Wind, glaciers, rockslides, and avalanches wear away at the rock; rivers carve deep gorges in the lower slopes as they trundle the debris away. When you approach Mount Everest, you are

Panoramic aerial shot of the East Face of Everest, taken by Leo Dickinson in 1991 from the first hot-air balloon to fly over the mountain. The twin peaks in the center of the picture are Lhotse (left) and Mount Everest, the notch between them is the South Col.

struck by the massive piles of rocky rubble that have built up around the base of the peak. A visitor to any of Everest's base camps can wander the heaps and river banks and pick up samples of most of the rocks that make up the mighty mountain: granite, gneiss, sandstone, and limestone.

All in all, this is a very unstable region. The pressure exerted by the Indian plate builds up energy underground, which eventually releases in the form of earth movements and earthquakes. It is not beyond the bounds of possibility that thousands of years from now Everest will be toppled by geological upset. Or, maybe, it will grow too high and collapse under the sheer force of gravity. Either way, some other mountain above the sea will then become the highest in the world. We like to say "as old as the hills," but hills do not last forever, not even the greatest and loftiest mountain of all.

TENZING NORGAY
NEPAL

1914–1986

First to reach summit of Everest with
Sir Edmund Hillary, May 29, 1953

Summit ascents: 1

On Top of the World

A story is told in the Sherpa valleys below Everest about how the great mountain known in Nepal as Sagarmatha came to be. Long, long ago, it runs, a huge cloud appeared in the sky, almost filling the universe. And from that cloud fell rain. For years and years it rained, and the rainwater remained suspended in space, a quivering lake held up by the force of the winds. These winds, which blew in from all directions of space, churned the surface of the water, churning and churning. In time, the churning produced a solid mass at the heart of the lake, which grew ever higher till it rose above the waters. The waves lapping at the sides of this new island became glaciers, and the falling rain turned into snow, covering it in a gleaming mantle. Thus, it is said, the Queen of Mountains was born, Sagarmatha, the crown jewel of the Earth.

After the deaths of Mallory and Irvine shocked the world, the summit of Everest remained elusive. Was this "crown jewel of the Earth" beyond the reach of humans?

WHEN TENZING NORGAY was growing up in the Sherpa homeland of Solu Khumbu, Mount Everest was a familiar presence. Sometimes he caught sight of it rising high into the sky over the tops of nearer mountains. In this Nepalese region of high peaks and valleys close to the border with Tibet, Tenzing was often sent into the mountains with his father's yaks. He liked to climb as high as he could, to 18,000 feet where the grass stopped and glaciers flowed down from the steep, stony mountain walls. The great peaks fascinated him, especially Everest—although that was not a name he recognized at the time. Locally, it was called Chomolungma. Usually, you see Chomolungma translated as "Goddess Mother of the World," but Tenzing said that where he lived Sherpa mothers taught their children that it was "The Mountain So High No Bird Can Fly Over It." All his life that was the name he loved best for the mountain he loved best.

Sherpas, as a people, originated in Tibet and crossed the main ridge of the Himalaya into Nepal about 450 years ago. They settled in the upper valleys to the south and west of Everest. Their language remains very similar to Tibetan, and they retain close contact with Tibetans across the border. There is evidence that Tenzing, the most famous Sherpa of all, was not born in the Sola Khumbu, but in Tibet. Nevertheless he grew up in the Sherpa village of Thame, the 11th of his family's 13 children.

It was not unusual for young Sherpas to travel widely to find work; some went down to Kathmandu, the capital of Nepal, others to the Indian Himalayan town of Darjeeling. Tenzing first ran away seeking adventure at the age of 13, but he grew homesick and returned to his parents after six weeks. But in 1932, when he was 18, he ran off again with other boys and girls from his village who wanted to earn money and to "see the world."

This time, he crossed into India and eventually reached Darjeeling. It was common knowledge that British mountaineers had been making attempts to climb Mount Everest and were employing Sherpas to help them. The next expedition, he learned, would be coming in 1933, and he desperately hoped to find work as a porter for the visiting climbers. To his great disappointment, he was not chosen, but in 1935, when another party came, he was selected to go. And after that, over the years, he took part in no less than seven attempts to climb Everest.

There were no official expeditions during the 1940s because of the Second World War and its aftermath. One unofficial attempt took place in 1947 when a Canadian, Earl Denman, traveling alone, hired two Sherpas to take him secretly into Tibet. Tenzing was one of these Sherpas, and he led the man to the slopes of the North Col. But with no special clothing or equipment they could climb no higher and were back in Darjeeling within five weeks.

When expeditions restarted in earnest, much had changed in the world. Communist China had occupied Tibet and no outsiders were allowed into that country. It would be three decades before western mountaineers could return. This meant that Everest was no longer accessible from Darjeeling. The only hope of climbing it now was by way of its southern slopes lying in Nepal, for Nepal was at last opening its borders to the outside world. After years of seclusion it was

ED HILLARY (standing) assists Tenzing Norgay across a crevasse near Camp 3, just above the icefall. Three six-foot sections of aluminum ladder were necessary to bridge this great crevasse barring access into the Western Cwm.

"He's got three lungs. The higher he goes, the better he feels."

—A SWISS CLIMBER ON TENZING'S FITNESS ON EVEREST

an almost medieval land, with very few roads. The only motorcar was one belonging to the king.

In 1950 a small Anglo-American party trekked into the Sola Khumbu and got a good look at the Khumbu Icefall, an impressive cascade of broken ice that bars access to the Western Cwm and the higher slopes of Everest on this side of the mountain. Riddled with crevasses, it didn't look at all encouraging. Nevertheless, armed with aerial photographs and a new map, a British reconnaissance expedition the following year managed to climb through the icefall and were convinced that with special ladders to cross the larger crevasses, it would be possible to get a team of climbers through that way.

As all Everest expeditions up to this time had been by climbers from Britain and the Commonwealth, somehow it had not occurred to the British that this could change. It came as a great shock to discover that the mountain was already booked for 1952. Swiss mountaineers had been granted sole access in the spring before the wet monsoon season, and after it in the autumn. This was a blow: After a siege of three decades, there was a real possibility that success could slip away from the British. They immediately put in an application for 1953 and intensified preparations and planning. Meanwhile they could only bite their nails and wait.

Tenzing accompanied the Swiss. In the spring, with Raymond Lambert, he climbed to within 820 vertical feet of the summit and afterward would joke that if only they'd been able to brew up a cup of tea, they would have made it to the top. But on the night before their final climb, they'd been stiff with cold, for there were no sleeping bags and no cooking stove in their high camp. They'd spent the whole time slapping and rubbing each other to keep the circulation going. The next morning they could only climb slowly, in fits and starts. Tenzing found himself thinking of his home and family in Darjeeling and wondering if he'd see them again. It was still possible they could climb Everest, but could they get down? "I thought of Mallory and Irvine," he said afterward, "and how they had disappeared forever, on the other side of the mountain, at just about the height we must be at now....Then I stopped thinking. My brain went numb. I was just a machine that moved and stopped, moved and stopped, moved and stopped. Then we stopped and did not move again."

They turned back. In the fall of that year conditions prevented them from climbing even as high as they did in the spring. It had been a tremendous effort: Lambert and Tenzing's high point of 28,210 feet was a new world record.

So the British would get another try. Their leader, Col. John Hunt, threw himself wholeheartedly into building a happy, cohesive team and working out how to get tons of equipment—sufficient tents, food, and oxygen—in position up the mountain for two or three well-founded summit attempts in 1953. He put together a team of strong alpinists, including two climbers from New Zealand, Edmund Hillary and George Lowe. Hillary had taken part in the 1951 Everest reconnaissance, as had the team's doctor, Michael Ward. Even so, no one had the practical experience on this mountain that Tenzing had. He knew the ground almost to the summit. John Hunt appointed him "Sirdar," in charge of the porters, but clearly he would also be a valuable member of the climbing team.

Hillary
Step

Mount Everest
29,035 ft
8,850 m

South Summit
28,710 ft

Northeast Ridge

Camp 9
27,900 ft

Southeast Ridge

South Col

Camp 8
25,800 ft

N o r t h
F a c e

S o u t h w e s t
F a c e

Geneva
Spur

L h o t s e
27,890 ft
8,501 m

L h o t s e
F a c e

Camp 7
24,000 ft

North Col

West Ridge

Camp 6
23,000 ft

Camp 5
22,000 ft

Camp 4
21,200 ft

W e s t e r n   C w m

1953 Expedition

—— Tenzing and Hillary route

THE FIRST SUMMIT: Route of the first
ascent of Mount Everest via the Western Cwm,
the South Col, and the Southeast Ridge.
The border between Nepal and Tibet takes the
line of the West and Southeast Ridges. This has
become the standard route on Mount Everest,
climbed dozens of times each year. Because
of its scale, exposure, and the unpredictability
of conditions, it remains a serious undertaking.

Unlike most Sherpas, for whom working with expeditions is one of the few job opportunities available, Tenzing was a mountaineer by choice, with a burning ambition to stand on top of the world. This he shared with Ed Hillary. A beekeeper by profession, Hillary always said that you needed a measure of ruthlessness and selfishness to be a successful mountaineer. He and Tenzing were equally matched in determination. Nobody worked harder than they did to ensure the expedition's success, but Hillary knew that for him and Tenzing, success meant being on the summit personally. Sensing this, Hunt wisely paired the two men as a likely assault team. Hillary had reason to bless the decision when Tenzing's prompt response saved him from disaster one day after he'd fallen into a crevasse.

The party set out on foot in the second week of March from near Kathmandu. In 17 days they reached Tengboche, below Everest. The team spent two weeks getting used to the thin air at altitude and preparing the route to Base Camp at 17,900 feet at the foot of the Khumbu Icefall. Staging camps were set in and beyond the icefall and Advance Base Camp (Camp 4) was established at 21,200 feet in the Western Cwm. This magnificent high valley was known by the Swiss as the Valley of Silence.

Camp 5 was placed 800 feet higher at the foot of the Lhotse Face. From here, the route went up the face—with two more camps—before traversing across to the South Col, a desolate wind tunnel of blue ice and rubble separating Everest and Lhotse. Here, at 25,800 feet, Camp 8 was established on May 21 by Wilfrid Noyce and Annullu Sherpa. Ahead, the Southeast ridge of Everest climbs steeply toward the South Summit, which the climbers had to cross to reach the main summit. The previous year Tenzing and Lambert had stopped short of the South Summit.

On May 26 John Hunt and Da Namgyal Sherpa struggled upward and dumped loads for an assault camp to be placed as high as possible on the ridge. It would be from here that Hillary and Tenzing would launch their summit bid. But, meanwhile, two other members, Charles Evans and Tom Bourdillon, were making the first climbing attempt. By starting out from the col, these two had no real chance of getting all the way to the top and back in a day. (Today, climbers do cover that distance on their summit day, but it means setting out from the col toward midnight the day before.) Hunt's plan for Evans and Bourdillon must have been simply for them to open the route over the South Summit and get a sense of what lay ahead.

Evans's oxygen apparatus gave him trouble for most of that day, and the going proved trickier than expected. At 1 p.m. the two men scrambled onto the South Summit to see the final, narrow, corniced ridge switchbacking ahead with alarming drops on either side. They had beaten the record set by Tenzing and Lambert, but could not safely go any higher. When they finally made it back down to the col, they were utterly exhausted. With icicles hanging from their faces, they looked like strangers from another planet.

So it really was down to Hillary and Tenzing. Two days later George Lowe, Alf Gregory, and Ang Nyima assisted them in setting up a small tent at 27,900 feet that would become Camp 9. Tucked on a tiny split-level platform overhanging the tremendous Southwest Face, they were to pass an uncomfortable night here, but in what a spectacular setting!

ON TOP OF THE WORLD: In this panorama taken by Ed Hillary from the summit of Everest looking south, we see the jagged ridges of Makalu, 12 miles away (right), with Chomo Lonzo (left), and Kangchenjunga in the distance.

CROWNING ACHIEVEMENT. Tenzing stands at last on the summit of Everest. Flying from his ice ax are flags of the United Nations, Britain, and Nepal. Now he looked down on the summits of other giants—Lhotse, Nuptse, and Makalu. "It was such a sight as I had never seen before and would never see again," he said, "wild, wonderful, and terrible."

"Everything we could see for hundreds of miles was below us, except only the top of Kangchenjunga, far to the east—and the white ridge climbing on above us into the sky," Tenzing said.

They had raging thirsts, and Tenzing spent hours melting snow, first for lukewarm coffee, then lemon juice, and later soup. They ate sardines, biscuits, and tinned fruit, but the fruit was frozen so hard, they had first to thaw it out over the stove. They kept on all their clothes to try to keep warm and breathed a little oxygen to help them sleep. Even so, they passed the night dozing and waking. Sometime around 4 a.m. Hillary looked outside to see the makings of a perfect day. Stomping his feet to get his circulation going, Tenzing let out a whoop of delight when he spotted the Tengboche Monastery miles below in the blue shadows of the valley. It seemed a good omen. They drank more lemon juice, sucked on some sugar lumps, and nibbled biscuits while Hillary thawed out his frozen boots over the primus stove. At 6:30, wearing all the clothes they had with them, they crawled outside and hoisted on their oxygen sets. This would be the day—May 29, 1953—that would change the lives of everyone on the expedition. Although it was still dark on their ledge, the way ahead was bathed in sunlight, beckoning them upward.

"Let's go!" Hillary urged, and, grinning, Tenzing scrambled past him, kicking a long line of footsteps back up to the main ridge.

TENZING AND HILLARY relax with a cup of tea back in Camp 4 after their great climb. They had carried no radios, and the rest of the team had to wait until the two climbers returned to this camp to learn of their success. "I think there has never been such excitement in the history of the Himalayas," Tenzing wrote afterward. "Everybody embraced everybody. 'Is it really true?' Hunt kept saying over and over again. And then he hugged me again in joy."

"A few more whacks of the ice ax in the firm snow, and we stood on top."

—SIR EDMUND HILLARY

The snow crust demanded care. Hillary took over the lead and painstakingly packed down the snow in each foothold as he forged over the South Summit. Conditions improved. The two picked their way delicately along the virgin ridge, between the cornices overhanging the East Face and the abrupt drop of the Southwest Face. After an hour or more of steady going they came to a steep, rocky step, some 40 feet high. They had known to expect it from aerial photographs, but no one knew whether or not it could be climbed. Luckily, Hillary was able to wedge himself half into a crack where the snow had pulled away from the rock and wriggle upward. The obstacle is called the Hillary Step today.

Tenzing followed, and the pair continued their undulating progress along the summit ridge until, having passed the last corner, ahead lay only a snowy dome and, beyond it, the vast Plateau of Tibet.

"A few more whacks of the ice ax in the firm snow, and we stood on top," Hillary said later, unwilling to spell out that he had made it a few paces ahead of Tenzing. He sought to shake hands, but Tenzing was having none of that. Flinging his arms around his friend's shoulders, he thumped him vigorously on the back. It was 11:30 a.m. and the highest pinnacle of the world was at last trodden by human foot.

The Everest achievement, inextricably linked in history with the coronation of Queen Elizabeth II, was seen within the Commonwealth as heralding a new and glorious era. Nowadays, we are more likely to regard it as the last great adventure of the British Empire. Either way there was nothing foregone about the conclusion. Every success requires an element of blessing, but above all this was the result of a magnificent team effort grafted onto hard experience earned over three decades and a dozen expeditions.

Sherpas of Everest

It was fitting that one of the first two men to reach the summit of Everest was a Sherpa, for it is sure the mountain would not have been climbed at that time without the Sherpa contribution. Every step on Everest had been earned with Sherpa assistance. The demands placed on them had been heavy, and the price they paid was high. The first seven fatalities of Everest expeditions were Sherpas.

The Sherpa people of Nepal came originally from Kham in southeastern Tibet. Their name is a corruption of *sharpa,* meaning people from the east. About 450 years ago they began migrating over the high passes along the Tibetan border to settle in the upper valleys south and west of Everest. Later, some Sherpas moved on to Darjeeling in India to find casual work. By the end of the 19th century people were already discussing the possibility of scaling Mount Everest. The first Everest expeditions recruited Darjeeling Sherpas for high-altitude work, and Himalayan mountaineers have gone on employing Sherpas ever since. The word "Sherpa" has become synonymous with supreme strength and reliability in harsh conditions.

For their own part, most Sherpas found it hard to understand the visitors' passion for the frigid summits where life was in constant danger. Left to themselves they may never have climbed mountains when it wasn't necessary. Yet climbing proved a welcome source of employment, and

Sherpa porters approaching Base Camp at the end of the long march in. Their loads can weigh as much as 40 pounds.

they became proficient mountaineers with a justified pride in their achievements. Before long, senior Sherpas on an expedition often had more practical experience of the mountain they were climbing than their employers, although their opinions were not often sought.

High-altitude work is a hard way to make a living, and it is no wonder that wives often urge their husbands to give it up. Yet life is improving for the Sherpas as Sherpa lodges and teahouses spring up to meet increased demand from trekkers and climbers. Khumbu, the name the Sherpas give their land, may still be beyond the reach of the motorcar, but thanks to help from Sir Edmund Hillary and others, there are now schools, electricity, and medical care. Educated Sherpas have a choice these days when it comes to careers, and those who do choose to work as porters or guides have formed cooperatives and can expect better pay and working conditions than their parents received. Theirs is a society half traditional, half modern, and under conflicting pressures. Yet the Sherpas' resilience, industriousness, and adaptability, not to mention their physical, cultural, and Buddhist religious strength, should see them through a time of great change.

QU YINHUA, GONGBU, WANG FUZHOU
CHINA

First to climb the North Col/Northeast Ridge Route, 1960
Summit ascents: 2

Red Flag in the Summit Snow

News of the first ascent of Mount Everest swept around the world. Hillary and Tenzing became household names, and their faces smiled out from newspapers and magazines for months. But it's hard to be sure how much was known about the great climb just on the other side of the mountain. In Tibet—now part of Communist China— news and information were strictly controlled. We can be certain that government authorities in the Chinese capital of Beijing, known at the time as Peking, had been following the story keenly, for they would shortly contest the ownership of Mount Everest. The international boundary with Nepal, they claimed, placed Everest inside China in its entirety. The claim included parts of the Sherpa homeland of the Khumbu. However, after a year's dispute, Nepal and China signed a treaty that agreed their shared border should still run through the top of the mountain. Tibet remained out of bounds for visiting mountaineers, but Nepal continued to issue permits for the southern approach to Everest's mighty summit.

THE CHINESE HAD no long history of mountaineering, as had Europeans and North Americans, but the new People's Republic under Mao Zedong placed great emphasis on sports and wanted its sportsmen and women to attain world excellence. In 1955 China was approached by communist allies in the U.S.S.R. (or the Soviet Union, a group of republics that included present-day Russia) proposing their two nations cooperate on an ambitious program of mountain climbing. The Soviets offered to train a group of Chinese in basic techniques to get the project started, and the offer was gratefully accepted. The Chinese looked around for whom to send.

It wasn't a question of asking who wanted to go. Out of the blue one young man, XuJing, a schoolteacher, was summoned to his boss and told that China required him to work as a mountaineer. "But isn't that rather dangerous?" Xu asked. He couldn't see the point of climbing mountains. Nor was he happy to confine himself to a single activity when there were other sports he enjoyed. But his leader was firm, "No, the decision is taken; you must do it. You're off to the Soviet Union for four months." (As time passed, XuJing found he enjoyed the life, especially going into wild places, and he continued working for Chinese mountaineering until he retired decades later.)

The new mountaineers climbed several high peaks with the Soviets over the next couple of years. Then their allies proposed a joint attempt on Mount Everest, approaching from the north, through Tibet, as the early British expeditions had done. It was decided that a scouting party should go in first, in the fall of 1958, to get an idea of the problems involved. More Chinese mountaineers would be needed, and this is when forestry worker Qu Yinhua was recruited, along with Wang Fuzhou, who had just graduated as a geologist. Both men were 23 years old. They were taken to climb Pic Lenin, the second highest mountain in Soviet Russia, and from there they went on to join the Everest reconnaissance, led by XuJing. After investigating two different approaches, the climbers reported back in favor of the Northeast Ridge, the route Mallory had always championed. Its advantage over other possibilities was that it presented less snow and ice, and not so much difficult rock. Mr. Xu was conscious that at that time the Chinese were none too experienced at either.

The two nations agreed that the Chinese would be responsible for transport and all arrangements as far as the North Col, above which—where the real mountaineering started—the Soviets would take charge. The Chinese government even built a new road all the way to Base Camp. This would enable trucks to bring in stores and equipment and keep the teams supplied with fresh food throughout the expedition.

Then came a setback. Just as the climbers were about to depart in the spring of 1959, a revolution broke out in Tibet, and the whole enterprise had to be postponed. By 1960, when conditions were safe once more, political relations between the two communist superpowers had deteriorated. To the disappointment of mountaineers on both sides, the Soviets pulled out of the expedition.

This left the Chinese in a difficult position. Could they climb great Everest on their own without their partner's expertise?

CHINESE 1960 EXPEDITION members negotiate a crevasse on the North Col (top), and return in triumph to Lhasa on June 7, 1960.

Could they afford to? Economically, these were difficult times in China, and the Soviets had been going to provide and pay for all the necessary and expensive high-altitude equipment.

In the end, Chinese mountaineers were given more government funding, but it was made very clear to them that they were expected to succeed. Their job was to uplift the nation with their courage; and above all, not to lose face. Two trusted mountaineers were sent on a shopping spree to Europe. They bought eight tons of high-altitude gear—lightweight tents, stoves, sunglasses, ropes, oxygen apparatus, etc.—from Switzerland, France, West Germany, Sweden, and Great Britain. Meanwhile, an advance party was dispatched to Everest to install the first camps, ready for the climbers' arrival. Back in China, Mr. Xu put the remaining team members through their rigorous final training.

Toward the end of March 20, trucks rolled into Rongbuk, up the new road, delivering climbers to the tented village that was base camp. Zhou Zheng, a coach of China's mountaineering team, has written that "twenty tents provided dormitories, a canteen, a club, a conference room, a clinic, a power station and a radio shack, all of which were illuminated at night." Dances were held from time to time as were soccer matches. Outside entertainment, including films and folk dancers, was also brought in. "The whole camp was permeated with a cheerful atmosphere," Zhou said, while adding, "no one felt the solitude of a mountain dweller."

MOUNT EVEREST AT SUNSET: The North Face is seen slashed by the Norton
(or Great) Couloir. Everest's characteristic plume of blown snow streams from the summit.

By mid-May, six camps were in place up the mountain, and climbers had scouted as high as the foot of the notorious "Second Step," the major obstacle at 28,280 feet on the Northeast Ridge. Meteorologists were predicting a week of fine weather before the monsoon, but by now everyone was tired out. Some were sick, some injured, two men had died, causing morale to sink. Yet, if they were to go for the top, it had to be now. A message was received from Beijing, "Reach the summit at any cost!"

Wang Fuzhou got ready to climb. With him would go Liu Lianman (who used to be a firefighter), and a Tibetan climber, Gongbu. First they took part in an oath-swearing ceremony. Raising clenched fists in the air, they vowed not to come back until they had conquered Chomolungma. Then, waving good-bye to their comrades, they left Base Camp.

Qu Yinhua, the former forestry worker, followed a little later with some oxygen and a small movie camera. His orders were to film them at the top camp and then come down. A week later, however, on May 24, when the three left Camp 7 to climb the last 1,115 feet of the mountain, Qu went with them. Gongbu led to the foot of the Second Step. British Everesters in the 1930s had pronounced this 100-foot feature as "probably unclimbable." No one knew if Mallory and Irvine had managed to get up it.

The first section proved easy enough, up a wide crack onto a sloping snow terrace. It was the steeper 20-foot cliff above, where the crack narrowed, that presented obvious problems. There was no firm footing on the sloping ledge below the cliff, so the four men tried to build a step at the bottom with their rucksacks. That didn't

Mount Everest
29,035 ft
8,850 m

Second Step
28,280 ft

First Step
28,110 ft

Northeast Ridge

North Face

Great (Norton) Couloir

West Ridge

North Ridge

Changtse
(Bei Peak)

1960 Expedition

—— Chinese route

"MALLORY'S ROUTE": Chinese mountaineers in 1960 followed the line of the Northeast Ridge to Everest's summit, the route Mallory always recommended.

work. Then Liu Lianman banged a piton into the crack above his head and made four attempts to get higher, using this peg. Each time he fell off, and each time it took him a quarter of an hour to recover. Then Qu Yinhua had a couple of goes, and he fell off too. There simply were no footholds. What could be done? They didn't dare go back down, having sworn to succeed.

Yet however hard they looked, there didn't seem to be any alternative way up. Absolutely nothing. Dejectedly, they sat in the snow. Suddenly, Liu had a brainstorm. He remembered how sometimes in the fire service, they'd used "combined tactics" to climb into difficult places: One man would stand on another's back or shoulders in a kind of human ladder to gain height. Immediately, Liu crouched down and invited Qu Yinhua to clamber up onto him. Qu took off his heavily nailed boots before doing so. With supreme effort, Liu Lianman stood up.

Now Qu could reach higher, and he walloped in a second piton. This time he was able to climb the steep step. At the top he belayed himself to a rock and brought up his colleagues on the rope. They brought up his boots.

It had taken three hours to surmount the Second Step, and Qu's feet were dangerously frostbitten. All were exhausted; Liu particularly was utterly worn out. When he tried to walk, he kept falling over. And they were still hours from the summit. How could they go on with Liu in this state?

"You must," he told them. "I'll wait here; I'll be alright." And he tucked himself out of the wind, piling snow over his sleeping bag for insulation. Amazingly, he didn't contract frostbite during his long, lonely wait, but he was frightened he would die there, and he wrote a good-bye note to the others, saving the last of his oxygen for their return.

His three friends kept going throughout the night. At 4:20 a.m. on May 25 they finally made it to the top. By that time only Gongbu had any oxygen left, and that too soon ran out. It was impossible for Qu to shoot film in the star-studded darkness. Unfurling the Chinese flag, they placed it and a plaster model of China's national leader, Chairman Mao, on a great rock near the summit. Then they scribbled their signatures on a piece of paper, which they buried under a heap of stones. This took a matter of minutes, after which, cold and befuddled from oxygen starvation, they started the long climb down. Wang Fuzhou said afterward that they slid back down the snow slope, as if on skis, knowing this was a dangerous thing to do. "We were so excited," he explained, "skiing and crying, with tears rolling down our faces."

They were worried about Liu, but as day dawned they could see him in the distance, waving, and hurried down to tell him their news. He seemed remarkably well after his night out; indeed, now he was the freshest of the four, and able to help them. They wasted no time descending the Second Step, but by now it had begun snowing hard. Liu and Gongbu were the strongest, so they pushed ahead to get help, leaving the other two to follow at their own pace.

Qu's frostbite made it hard for him to walk, and his hands too were badly affected. Wang, confused from lack of oxygen, was becoming argumentative. He thought he was going down even when standing still, and was sure they were heading the wrong way.

In fact, these two had a nightmarish few days of it, which they were lucky to survive. They were roped together, so when Qu slipped, they both went into a slide, which was stopped only when they ran into stones. In the fall, Wang lost a boot and was forced to wrap his foot in extra socks and a mitten. Ironically, this foot stayed well protected, while the other suffered bad frostbite because his boot was too tight. There was no one in Camp 6 when they reached it, and the tents were buried under snow. They kept going, finally bivouacking in their sleeping bags at about 26,250 feet. The next night, at the camp on the North Col, they at last found some stores and didn't have to rely on snow alone to eat. They were able to snatch some sleep. On the afternoon of the following day team members met them and assisted them down, reaching Advance Base Camp on the 28th. From there, they were carried the 12 miles into Base Camp.

Qu later had all his frostbitten toes and parts of his feet, as well as six fingers, amputated. Wang lost five toes and the top joints of four fingers. The men were almost unrecognizable from weight loss. When the rest of the team returned to Beijing for triumphal celebrations, these two were left in a hospital in Lhasa, Tibet, and only got home again in the middle of September.

Were Qu, Wang, and Gongbu the first to have reached the summit

of Everest from the north? Did they think Mallory and Irvine could have reached the summit by that route? When asked this question, Qu said he simply didn't know. Somewhat bitterly he added that he hoped not, or all his suffering would have been in vain.

News of the Chinese achievement was greeted with disbelief by many Westerners. It seemed inconceivable that climbers from a country with only five years' mountaineering experience could succeed on a climb that had defeated the best alpinists of earlier generations. There were no photographs to prove they had been to the top. Shots from Qu's film were scrutinized closely, but no one could agree that any were taken above the critical Second Step, and many people doubted they could possibly have climbed that obstacle. As it happens, Qu did have one picture from above the Second Step. At dawn, on his way down, he had looked back and taken a short, shaky shot of the summit, bathed in sunshine. Unfortunately, no one in the 1960s could interpret this, as no other images were available for comparison. Decades later Jochen Hemmleb, a German historian, was able from subsequent photographs to reliably identify where Qu must have been standing at the time. In 1975 Chinese mountaineers went to the top once more—undisputably, this time. They left a tripod on the summit for others to find, and fixed a metal ladder in the difficult upper section of the Second Step, which is maintained to this day.

Women on Everest

Women came late to Mount Everest, even though one of the first people to speculate about climbing the peak was a woman. The American Meta Brevoort wrote about the possibility of an Everest expedition during the summer of 1876: "No fear of wild beasts, nor rains at the proper season, nor hostile natives if one could get properly accredited." It might prove too high, she conceded, but with an enviable climbing record in the Alps she remained gloriously undaunted. At the time she was already almost 50 years old, and unfortunately died rather suddenly later that year, before her plans bore any fruit.

A French woman was bold enough to apply to join the team that went to Everest in 1924, only to be told very firmly by the astonished British organizers that no ladies of whatever nationality could possibly be included. The difficulties would be too great. Some Tibetan women were employed as porters by those early expeditions, but they did not go high. The Chinese included a handful of women among the 200-plus members who took part in their 1960 Everest expedition, but they, too, were not allowed beyond the foot of the North Col.

Things began to change in 1975 (the United Nations-designated Year of the Woman), when on May 16 a Japanese music teacher and scientific journalist became the first female to reach the summit. She climbed the standard route via the South Col. Junko Tabei was was 35 years old, married, and the mother of a young daughter. She was part of an all-female expedition employing male Sherpas. Incredibly, within 11 days, another woman stood on top of Everest. Phantog (or Panduo, as her name is sometimes written), was a 37-year-old Tibetan mother of three, and she went to the summit with eight male companions, via the northern side. She was deputy leader of a 400-strong Chinese expedition and one of 15 women members to climb above 25,500 feet. The team carried oxygen, but reportedly took only "minimal inhalings" to refresh themselves.

Today more than 70 ascents can be claimed by women. Nevertheless, women still make up less than 5% of Everest's summiters. To date, five women have died on Everest, four of them while descending from the top. Two women have climbed Everest from both sides, the South African Cathy O'Dowd and Lhakpa Sherpa from Nepal; and two others—Kui Sang of China and the Indian Santosh Yadav—have repeated ascents by the same route. The first American women to stand on top of the world were Stacey Allison from Colorado and Peggy Luce of Seattle; they both climbed the South Col route in the fall of 1988. Most women have used supplementary oxygen during their climbs, except Lydia Bradey (New Zealand) and the British climber Alison Hargreaves. Hargreaves, in fact, made her 1995 ascent of the North Face/Northeast Ridge unsupported above Base Camp. She would not accept so much as a cup of tea from other climbers, wanting to be totally independent. Although Everest is too busy these days for a pure solo ascent (such as Reinhold Messner made in 1980), Hargreaves's achievement is the nearest equivalent. Mother of two small children, this remarkable climber died a few months later when she was blown off the world's second highest mountain, K2, on the border of China and Pakistan.

Junko Tabei triumphant. The 35-year-old from Japan became the first woman ever to reach the top of Everest on May 16, 1975. She is seen here descending with Ang Tsering Sherpa, who guided her to the top from the South Col.

REINHOLD MESSNER
ITALY

First ascent of Everest without oxygen in 1978,
and the first solo ascent in 1980

Summit ascents: 2

Everest by "Fair Means"

Throughout the history of high-altitude mountaineering, climbers have had mixed feelings about using oxygen apparatus to help them breathe in the thin air. Was it cheating? No one knew at the beginning what the body's limits were. If it turned out that Everest rose too high for anyone to breathe unaided on the summit, then there'd be no choice but to use it. In any case, was giving your body the amount of oxygen it needed really any different from eating high-energy food? If it allowed you to climb higher, what could be the harm?

The arguments went round and round. George Mallory had been against using oxygen, yet he changed his mind when it seemed that Mount Everest would never be climbed without it. In 1953 there was no question in John Hunt's mind: Climbers on his expedition would breathe extra oxygen on the upper slopes, and they would also use it to aid sleep. Team members had no choice in the matter. Neither, it turned out, did they have any complaints. That pretty well remained the position for another 20 years.

REINHOLD MESSNER IS one of those climbers who has made a habit of proving the "impossible" can sometimes be possible. He hated the way Himalayan expeditions loaded themselves with ever more equipment, just to make life easier. To his mind, this upset the fine balance between man and mountain, taking away some of the adventure. If you employed hundreds of porters to carry your stores, he said, and banged in metal pegs to get you up steep rock and ice; and, above all, if you sucked oxygen from a cylinder while you were climbing— then you were effectively shrinking the mountain. The more he thought about it, the more Messner found himself wondering if bottled oxygen was really necessary to get up Mount Everest. Could it be that the world was constructed so that people could move freely around it, and even climb to its highest point without mechanical aids? He longed to be able to prove that and began nursing the ambition to climb Mount Everest, as he put it, by "fair means."

Reinhold Messner was the second of nine children of a South Tyrolean schoolmaster and his wife. He was born in 1944. South Tyrol is a mountainous Alpine region, which has belonged to Italy since the end of the World War I. Before that, it was Austrian, and most of the population, like Reinhold himself, still speak German. A strong characteristic of the South Tyroleans is a fiercely independent spirit.

Reinhold's father, a keen climber in his youth, introduced all his children to the mountains. One of Reinhold's most precious memories is of the day when, as a five-year-old, he made his first climb. He went with his parents and his older brother up the Geislerspitze near their summer home in the mountains. It was a revelation to him, the beginning of his lifelong passion. As a teenager, he used to go off climbing with his next younger brother—Günther. By the time he was 18, Reinhold had repeated some of the hardest rock climbs around and had tackled Alpine ice. He and Günther even climbed with talented older climbers on routes no one had tried before.

Eventually, Reinhold felt confident in attempting difficult climbs on his own. Solo climbing is often frowned upon as it is seen to carry more risk than roped climbing. Even so, there have always been those who enjoy the intensity of climbing without companions. It brings you face to face with your strengths and weaknesses. And knowing your abilities, Messner always believed, was the strongest safety factor. You could move faster on your own, take advantage of the moment.

"Don't carry your courage in your rucksack," Messner urged all those who climbed with pegs and hammers and a spider's web of ropes and tackle. "Don't kill off the impossible." What you can't do by fair means should be left for another generation, he said. And that went for climbing Himalayan summits, too. At the time he hadn't climbed beyond the European Alps himself, but that was about to change. In 1969 Reinhold and Günther were invited to join a large German expedition attempting the steep Rupal Face of Nanga Parbat in the Punjab Himalaya.

After weeks of effort, the brothers reached the top together but were forced to bivouac high on the mountain without shelter. By morning Günther was weak and altitude sick, and he felt unable to return by the difficult way they'd come up. The brothers decided to risk descending the other side of the mountain, which they hoped would prove easier, even though there'd be no camps or comrades.

THE DANGEROUS KHUMBU ICEFALL, where many people have been killed by collapsing ice. In 1978 Reinhold Messner and Peter Habeler preferred to scoot through this section unroped, reasoning that it would be easier to leap to safety if an ice tower suddenly crashed down.

PLOUGHING THROUGH DEEP SNOW under the scorching heat of midday is backbreaking work, but in retrospect Messner says even trailblazing contributed to the reward he sought: stripping down to essentials and achieving balance within himself.

"I want to climb until either I reach the top of the mountain, or I can go no further…. I'm prepared to endure anything, to risk much. I am willing to go further than ever I have before…to stake everything I have."

—REINHOLD MESSNER

It ended in tragedy. At the foot of the face, Günther, who had fallen behind, disappeared. For a day and a night Reinhold searched for him before having to accept that his brother must have died under an avalanche and was lost forever. Devastated, he came home to spend weeks in the hospital with frostbite. Six of his toes were amputated.

Gradually Messner recovered. In time he went back to the Himalaya, still bent on his dream. In 1975, with Peter Habeler, an Austrian friend, he climbed the world's 11th highest mountain, Hidden Peak, in lightweight style—no oxygen apparatus and no porters on the mountain. The two were up and down in five days.

Three years later he and Habeler attached themselves to an Austrian Everest expedition. The other members were attempting the South Col/Southeast ridge in the normal way: pre-stocking camps, fixing ropes, breathing bottled oxygen. Reinhold and Peter played their parts—carrying loads, building camps, and breaking trail—while rejecting the use of oxygen. They wanted to find out once and for all if the clumsy cylinders were vital for reaching the summit.

Many people considered their chance of success slim; some even predicted brain damage if they spent much time in the oxygen-starved atmosphere up there. The scoffers made them more determined to see how high they could get. On the evening of May 7, the two men were camped on the South Col, poised for a make-or-break bid the next day. It was a perfect evening and they felt confident.

By 3 a.m. they were up, melting snow for drinks. Two or three hours later they left their tent, to be stung in the face by a sleety squall. Pressing on, into desolate emptiness, it was impossible for them to tell what was mountain and what was sky. Occasional breaks in the clouds confirmed that they were keeping to the right line. Where the East Face drops away on one side and the Southwest Face on the other, they roped together, taking turns leading along the tricky, narrow ridge linking them with the summit. Reinhold stopped frequently to take photographs or to film. Sometimes he didn't remember to replace his goggles when he finished, a mistake for which he paid later with a bad bout of snow blindness. For the moment, though, concentration was focused on that little point ahead, where all the lines come together—the summit, the apex of their universe!

And they made it! Just after 1 p.m. they stood on the highest point on Earth, hugging one another and crying like babies. Their breath came in rasping gulps, but they were breathing—breathing this thin, meager air—the first men ever to climb Everest without oxygen bottles and face masks. Despite Reinhold's snow blindness, they got down safely, with their brain cells intact.

That sounds like the end of the story, yet there is more. Success prompted Messner to push his theories one step further. If you can climb Everest without oxygen and without Sherpas, then can you do so without any companion at all? Within months of his climb with Habeler, Messner disappeared for Nanga Parbat and set off alone up the West Face. All that first day (August 6) and the next, he climbed. On August 8, he woke early to the roar of avalanches. An earthquake was rattling the mountain, wiping away the track he had just come up. Yet he kept climbing, and on the afternoon of the next day he was standing on Nanga Parbat's summit for the second time, having completed a brand-new route on the Diamir Face, entirely on his own.

By 1980 he felt ready for the Big One. With his girlfriend Nena

Mount Everest
29,035 ft
(8,850 m)

First Step 28,110 ft

Second Step 28,280 ft

Northeast Ridge

North Face

West Ridge

North Ridge

Great (Norton) Couloir

Messner's second bivouac
August 19th

Changtse
(Bei Peak)

Messner's first bivouac
August 18th

1980 Climb

—— Reinhold Messner
first solo ascent

MAN VERSUS MOUNTAIN: For his solo ascent of Everest, Reinhold Messner drew inspiration from the North Face traverse made by Norton and Somervell in 1924. Climbing the Great (Norton) Couloir to the summit, he avoided the obstacle of the Second Step. Messner's first oxygenless ascent of Everest with Peter Habeler was from the other side of the mountain (not shown), by the South Col-Southeast Ridge route.

PETER HABELER, AT 28,870 FEET with the difficult Hillary Step behind him, tackles the final corniced ridge to the summit.

"One alone is enough if...he is prepared to accept the possibility that in the last resort, if things go really wrong, he will die."

—REINHOLD MESSNER

Holguin, he trekked to the Tibetan side of Everest. Nena waited for him at Advance Base Camp at the top of the East Rongbuk Glacier as Messner followed in the footsteps of the 1920s pioneers. He did not intend to take Mallory's Northeast Ridge, which the Chinese climbed in 1960 and 1975. Instead, he would trek across the North Face, as Norton attempted to do in 1924.

He had chosen mid-August for this attempt, which is during the monsoon when there is a lot of snow on the mountain. Carrying his tent, sleeping bag, stove, fuel, food, and climbing equipment, he set off. Within minutes, he and his 33-pound pack had fallen into a crevasse. This could easily have spelled the end of the venture—and of Reinhold—but he scrambled out and still managed to reach the North Col in record time. All that day he climbed steadily and easily before bivouacking at 25,590 feet. Next day he traversed the North Face diagonally to the Norton Couloir, altitude and fatigue taking their toll. Sometimes he felt he couldn't go on; his body screamed to stop, to go back down, but he drove himself upward. That night he camped on a rocky outcrop out of the wind at the foot of the couloir. He scooped up pan after pan of snow to make lukewarm drinks. When he woke he felt "just as tired as the evening before, and stiff as well." "Now or never," he told himself firmly. If he was not going up, he would have to go down. Staying to rest was too dangerous. Okay, he would go—but he'd leave his rucksack and tent there. He buckled on his crampons, picked up his camera and short ax, and started climbing. His pulse was racing at more than 100 beats a minute.

He had a strange feeling that someone was with him. He'd been hearing voices in the air on and off for a while. Sometimes he talked

to a mystery companion, sometimes to the ice ax. He was not alarmed by this bizarre behavior; he had had a similar experience on Nanga Parbat—it must be connected with fatigue and lack of oxygen. The couloir got very steep and he left it for the unpleasantly exposed slabs to the right. It was a fight to keep his concentration, but a slip here would have been disastrous. For hours, he forced himself onward until late in the afternoon he spotted the Chinese tripod. He made it! But where was the joy, the pride of achievement? He felt empty, like stone. Wanting nothing more than to sit and melt away, he made himself take photographs. Then he turned wearily back toward his little tent, reaching it just before dark.

He couldn't bring himself to cook or eat, and there was no sleep to be had—just a wrenching high-altitude cough. When morning came he abandoned the tent and sleeping bag and headed down. All day long he trudged down, down, down beyond the North Col, all the way down, till he saw Nena on the glacier below, waiting and watching.

"He looked like a drunken man," Nena said afterward. She ran out to meet him and led him into the tent. Putting ice packs on his forehead, she poured can after can of fruit juice into his dehydrated body.

He'd been to his very limits, and he'd survived. Now he knew: One man could climb Everest completely alone, without extra oxygen. From bottom to top and back again—by fair means. The irony was that as Everest grew more popular, no other person, man or woman, would have an empty mountain to themselves as he had.

Everest's Altitude

When we talk of thin air at high altitude, we don't mean that the composition of air changes up high. The percentage of oxygen stays the same as at sea level: almost 21%. It is the air pressure that decreases the higher you go. So each lungful of air you swallow contains less oxygen. The air contains less of all its ingredients—it is simply spread more thinly. At a height of 15,750 feet only half the amount of oxygen is available for breathing as at sea level, and on the summit of Everest only one-third.

Acclimatization—the body's efforts to adapt to a potentially dangerous atmosphere—is necessary at high altitudes and cannot be rushed. The mountaineers' golden rule is to build up to new heights slowly—"Climb high, sleep low." Give your body a chance to get used to each level. It is not an exact science. Individuals vary widely in their tolerance and acclimatization powers. And for everyone there is a limit to what can be adjusted to—even following all the precautions. Nowhere in the world do humans live permanently above about 17,500 feet. Above 21,000 feet is often referred to as the "Death Zone." To spend time at this altitude is inevitably damaging. "You die a little every day" is another climbers' saying.

Most people experience headaches and perhaps feel nauseous when they first climb higher than they are accustomed to. They are breathless, and they have no appetite. That usually clears up, if they are ascending slowly. But above, say, 12,000 feet, there are two very serious conditions to watch out for—and for both the only safe treatment is to get lower fast. High-altitude pulmonary edema (HAPE) and high-altitude cerebral edema (HACE) can be fatal within hours. In HAPE there is a buildup of fluid in the lungs—often heard as a bubbling or crackling in the chest—and this can ultimately "drown" the climber. First symptoms might be extreme shortness of breath, a wet cough, headaches, and hallucinations, or a blueness around the face and fingernails. The same bluish look could indicate HACE, which is a swelling of the brain—again brought about by excessive fluid. This causes pressure within the skull, which can bring about a stroke or paralysis or disturb your eyesight. In this case, first signs might be awkwardness, irritability, or irrational behavior.

Nowadays, most expeditions carry a "Gamov Bag" or a similar kind of portable pressure chamber. With the patient sealed inside, it can be operated by a foot pump to simulate lower altitude, thus buying time for the patient, but it remains urgent to get them down the mountain.

Another serious effect of not getting enough oxygen is that your brain gets fuddled. Your reasoning and decision making are not as reliable as they should be, yet you may remain convinced you are your normal alert self. Who knows how many slips and falls, or bad judgements at altitude, or simply being in the wrong place at the wrong time, have lack of oxygen as their cause?

Other things to guard against up high include snow blindness, frostbite, weight loss, and sleeplessness. You may wonder why anyone climbs high mountains at all! Climbers such as Reinhold Messner and Peter Habeler have shown that for short periods, acclimatized humans can live and operate in the Death Zone, but they must not linger up there or their lives will be in grave danger.

In 1924 porter Namgya suffered frostbitten fingers from the extreme cold. It wasn't as bad as it looks and he later recovered fully. There are various degrees of frostbite, but at its worst it affects the extremities and is irreversible. Victims can lose parts of their hands and feet and even their noses.

1983 TEAM
UNITED STATES

**First to summit Everest
from the East side,
October 1983**

Kangshung Face: The East Side Story

As more climbers came to Mount Everest, new routes were traced up its rugged slopes. Ridgelines offered the most straightforward passage and were climbed first. The Southeast Ridge yielded to Hillary and Tenzing in 1953, and the Northeast Ridge to the Chinese seven years later. Americans claimed the next prize when, in 1963, they climbed a significant section of the West Ridge. Only then did climbers start looking at Everest's great faces.

The Tibetan side of the mountain remained off limits to foreigners from 1939 until the early 1980s, putting two of these three faces out of bounds. So it was the steep Southwest Face that was conquered first—despite a formidable rock band crossing the face above 26,000 feet—by an expedition led by British climber Chris Bonington in September 1975. Then, in the spring of 1980, the Japanese climbers Tsuneoh Shigehiro and Takashi Ozaki made the first full ascent of the North Face. That left just one face remaining, the largest of all.

Fearsomely steep and draped in snow and ice, Everest's East, or Kangshung, Face was dismissed by George Mallory during his reconnaissance of 1921. It would be suicidal to attempt it, he considered, describing how a huge glacier overhung the face, menacing the rocks below:

> *it required but little further gazing to know that almost everywhere ...must be exposed to ice falling from this glacier;...the perform-ance would be too arduous, would take too much time and would lead to no convenient platform; that, in short, other men, less wise, might attempt this way if they would, but emphatically it was not for us.*

The "other men, less wise" did not put in an appearance for 60 years. When the Chinese began letting outsiders back into Tibet in 1980, among the first to arrive were some American mountaineers heading for the Chinese peak of Gongga-Shan. One of them, Andrew Harvard, made a side trip into Tibet after that climb to take a good look at the Kangshung Face. Was it really as hopeless as Mallory judged it?

A three-day truck ride from the Tibetan capital of Lhasa brought him to the roadhead of Kharta. Here, Harvard hired a couple of yak herders to guide him to the Kangshung Glacier under the East Face. It was an exciting trek through dense rhododendron forests, across alpine meadows, over high passes, and into secret valleys. Halfway through the third day, the little party rounded a corner and there before them was the daunting Kangshung Face.

"Nothing prepared me for that view," Harvard wrote later. "I suddenly faced an immense mass of ice and rock thrusting toward the vault of the sky. For many moments I stood motionless at the majesty of the scene—the virtually unknown East Face of Mount Everest."

As he watched, an avalanche broke away from the glacier high on the mountain wall, still a dozen or so miles away. "Gathering size and speed as it descended the face, the slide spilled down and over the great buttresses of rock, exploding in a cloud of atomized ice on the surface of the Kangshung Glacier."

That was always going to be the problem with this overladen, two-mile-high face: He could see exactly what Mallory meant. With so much ice poised up there, it took only the slightest trigger—be it more snow, wind, a change of temperature, or falling rock—to send it crashing down. There would be very little warning. By the time you heard an avalanche's rumble, or felt its airblast, it would be too late.

For two days Harvard sat watching the sunlight shift across the face. In the changing light and shadow, its features slowly revealed themselves. Five long ribs or ridges of rocks, pinched together like fingers, reached down toward the Kangshung Glacier. Above them, a formless jumble of ice and snow gathered in the scoop of the upper face. This unstable mass—Mallory's hanging glacier—was the source of the constant avalanches. Harvard could see cracks and ledges that might be linked together into a route up there. Most important, he detected a subtle ridgeline mounting these upper slopes. If climbers could keep to the crest of that, he believed, they'd be above the reach of the avalanches' broad sweep.

"It would be difficult and dangerous," he reported back to the American Alpine Club, "but not impossible, not suicidal." Without any doubt it was the greatest challenge left on Mount Everest.

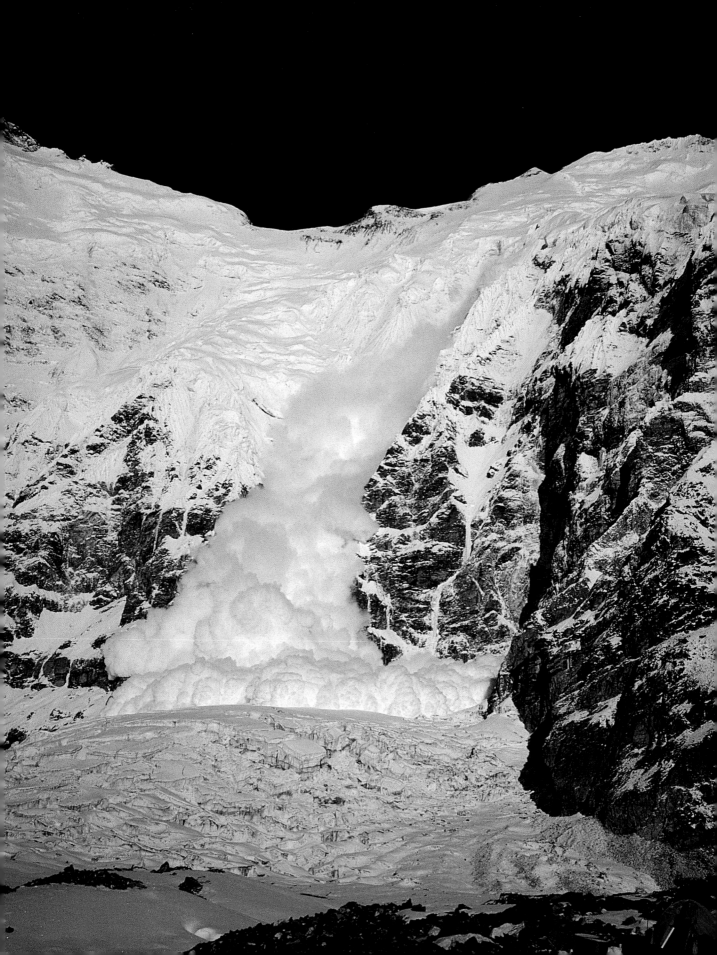

AVALANCHE! Tons of snow thunders down Everest's Kangshung Face. Since climbers first ventured onto the world's highest mountain in 1921, avalanches have been the major killer. By the year 2000 49 people had died the White Death on Everest.

At the end of August 1981, the first mountaineering team arrived, a group of big-name American climbers led by Richard Blum of San Francisco. Lou Reichardt was climbing leader, and the Chinese liaison officer accompanying the party was none other than Wang Fou Zhou, who'd climbed Everest in 1960. Harvard was one of the team, and Sir Edmund Hillary joined them, too—not as a high climber, but to give advice from Base Camp.

The first task facing the expedition was to climb an enormous rocky buttress that would lead them from the glacier onto the southernmost of the "finger-ridges." This, in turn, would deliver them to the snowfields above and Harvard's "subtle ridgeline." Easier said than done, however. It was a shock to find themselves confronted with a complicated 4,000-foot climb up difficult, often vertical rock, broken by knife-edged snow ridges.

For a month and a half they labored over Lowe Buttress, as it became known for the selfless efforts of George Lowe who did the bulk of this exploratory work. One section was called the "Bowling Alley." It was a tilted corridor, threatened from above by a fringe of 50-foot icicles. Chunks of rock and ice whizzed down it regularly. These were the bowling balls; the climbers were the bowling pins.

At last three camps were set up, linked by fixed ropes. The highest, on top of the buttress, they called Helmet Camp. At 21,500 feet, it put them in position, so they hoped, to attack the upper slopes.

THE SERENITY OF THE EAST FACE as reflected in this pond on the Kharta Glacier gives small indication of the treacherous climbing slopes on this side of Everest.

PRECARIOUSLY PERCHED ON LOWE BUTTRESS, Pinsetter Camp occupied the narrowest of ledges beneath an overhang. This is 2,000 feet into the climb, with 9,200 feet more to go to the summit.

The camp was occupied for only one night, however, when a fierce storm blew in, and all the climbers pulled back to base.

By now, some of the team members were having misgivings. Perhaps this East Face route really was too hard and unacceptably dangerous. Several climbers were sick, suffering from a variety of breathing problems, stomach disorders, or minor injuries; all were exhausted after the rigors of the previous weeks. They held a meeting to discuss what should be done.

Early in October, those who remained eager returned to the fight. If they could move quickly, there was a slim chance that one or two pairs could yet make it to the top before winter set in. A lot of new snow had fallen, and the trails all had to be re-broken, the camps and supplies dug out. At last, in clear, cold weather, they were back on top of the Helmet. But big crevasses appeared to bar the way ahead, and the surface snow had a dangerous-looking texture. It hadn't settled firmly and threatened to crumble into what are known as slab avalanches. Prudently, though with great reluctance, Reichardt called off the expedition. The highest point they achieved had been 23,400 feet. Although that meant there were still more than 5,500 feet to go to the summit, they had climbed the hardest part of this route and vowed to come back and finish the job another year.

True to their word, August 1983 saw eight of these climbers back in Beijing and reunited with Wang Fou Zhou and the interpreter, Mr. Tsao. This time their leader was James Morrissey, and the team was boosted with six strong newcomers: Carlos Buhler, Jay Cassell, Dave Cheesmond, David Coombs, Chris Kopczynski, and Carl Tobin. It also included John Boyle, who was not a climber but had come in the unusual role of "expedition engineer."

He planned to fix a winch and hauling line that could convey heavy loads up the initial 4,000-foot Lowe Buttress. Such an aerial cableway, powered by a portable generator, proved too difficult to install for the full distance. Instead, Boyle and Cassell constructed two shorter hauling systems up the steepest sections. Such mechanical assistance was controversial, and not all the team approved of its use. Nor did it prove a speedier solution than ferrying up loads on climbers' backs. But climbers were certainly fresher by the time they arrived at Helmet Camp—and could comfort themselves that in 1981, members had lugged their equipment up here manually.

By the end of September all 13 climbers were safely settled at Helmet Camp with 2,000 pounds of stores. This became Advance Base Camp, from which teams of three, four, or five men took turns breaking trail and pushing the route upward. In this way three more camps were set up, the highest at 25,800 feet. It had a glorious view, looking out over Tibet to the north and toward beautiful Kangchenjunga to the east.

On October 7 Buhler, Kim Momb (back from the 1981 team), and Reichardt tucked into this high camp and boosted their calories and liquid intake. They woke at three a.m. and, moving slowly in the thin air, were out of the tent in knee-deep snow by 4:30.

Lhotse
27,890 ft
8,501 m

Mount Everest
29,035 ft
8,850 m

South Summit
28,710 ft

Northeast Ridge

South Col

Camp 3
25,800 ft

KANGSHUNG
FACE
(East Face)

Camp 2
25,000 ft

Camp 1
23,500 ft

Helmet Camp
21,500 ft

Snow Camp
19,000 ft

Pinsetter Camp
20,000 ft

Route behind moraine

Advanced Base Camp
17,650 ft

Kangshung Glacier

1983 Expedition

—— American route

EVEREST'S MOST DIFFICULT FACE:
Route of the first ascent of Everest's Kangshung
(East) Face, which joins the Southeast Ridge in
its upper stages. Reconnoitered in 1981 and
climbed by an American team in the fall of
1983, this steep and potentially dangerous line
has never been repeated.

After six hours of very heavy slogging, the three broke out onto the Southeast Ridge of Everest at 27,800 feet. They had now joined the standard route, coming up from Nepal via the South Col, and there was a group of men climbing ahead of them who had come up that way. They were members of a Japanese party making an oxygenless ascent, and the Americans quickly overtook them.

From here, the going was easier, or at least the snow conditions were better. The gradient of the slope approaching the South Summit was far steeper than the Americans had expected. However, they moved well and reached the summit in calm weather at 2:30 that afternoon. The mountain had been climbed at last by the East Face.

These three descended safely, which is more than can be said for the group they had met earlier. Two of the Japanese and a Sherpa did not survive that day. On October 9, three more of the East Face team made it to the top: George Lowe, Jay Cassell, and Dan Reid. But a third attempt by other members a few days later had to be abandoned when another fierce storm blew in from Nepal and India. The last of the team members withdrew from the mountain in foul winter weather, new snow avalanching around them.

They were lucky to retreat without mishap. This climb has never been repeated. One other route has been traced on the East Face, avoiding the daunting initial Lowe Buttress.

Records on Everest

There are obvious "firsts" in the history of climbing a mountain—first to the summit, first without oxygen, first for his or her country. These are records that everyone can recognize; but once they have been set, what remains for others to achieve?

Anyone's first time up Everest is of course a great personal achievement, but it may not necessarily be seen as special by other people. It's more exciting to be the oldest or youngest, the fastest or the most innovative. Besides the thrill of making it into the record books, it must not be forgotten that climbing Mount Everest is an expensive business. Most people are obliged to seek sponsorship and publicity to get their ventures off the ground. To attract either, your likelihood of success is greater if you are planning something newsworthy or novel—or simply preposterous.

One example is coming down Everest on skis. This was first attempted by the Japanese ski-mountaineer Yuichiro Miura in the spring of 1970. Descending the Lhotse Face from the South Col, this skier achieved a reported speed of 93 mph, using a parachute to slow himself down at the end of his run. In 1992 Pierre Tardivel of France skied down 10,500 feet from the South Summit, achieving the longest ski run in the world to that date. Then in 1996 Hans Kammerlander from South Tyrol, after a very swift ascent of the north side, strapped on his skis on the top of the mountain. Apart from a few rocky sections, which he estimated all together totalled little more than 800 vertical feet, he skied all the way back to base in less than seven hours. The whole round trip had taken him less than 24 hours. You would have thought that descent record hard to beat, yet four years later, Davo Karnicar from Slovenia came to the the southern side of Everest in the post-monsoon season. With more snow than Kammerlander had, he was able to make his 2 ½ mile descent nonstop. Wearing custom-made skis, it took him only five hours.

Then there are the snowboarders and people with hang gliders and those with paragliders. In 1991 two hot-air balloons flew over the summit of Everest, a highly dangerous enterprise.

There have been family quests—sons and grandsons following in the footsteps of their forebears. Edmund Hillary's son, Peter, climbed Everest in 1990. In 1995 George Mallory's grandson (bearing the same name) completed the route where the first George lost his life 71 years before. One of Tenzing's sons and a grandson have repeated his climb, making what is believed the first three-generation success. Husbands and wives have climbed Everest together to clasp hands on top; and fathers and sons and brothers.

For some the challenge of climbing Everest is not enough by itself. Tim Macartney-Snape, having already participated in one of the boldest first ascents on the mountain, climbed Everest again in 1990—starting at sea level. From the Bay of Bengal, he walked the 620 miles to Base Camp before making his climb. Göran Kropp preferred to arrive by bicycle. He set off from Sweden by bike, carrying all he needed for an Everest climb, and pedaled to Base Camp before climbing the mountain and biking home. People can be quite inventive in hunting out firsts.

Extreme skier Davo Karnicar from Slovenia took less than five hours to come down Everest in October 2000. Hundreds of thousands of people in more than 70 countries witnessed his descent on the Internet.

SCOTT FISCHER
UNITED STATES

Professional Guide
Mountain Madness

Summit ascents: 2

ROB HALL
NEW ZEALAND

Professional Guide
Adventure Consultants

Summit ascents: 5

Everest for Everyone?

Back in the 1950s just one expedition per year was permitted on the Nepalese side of Everest. Later, this became one expedition per climbing route per season, each spring and fall. As demand increased two more seasons were introduced—winter and during the monsoon. Rules were relaxed further to allow several teams on any one route at the same time. Visiting expeditions are charged peak fees to climb, and for Nepal, one of the world's poorest nations, its mountains are an important source of revenue, besides providing much-needed local jobs.

A phenomenon of the mid-1980s was the emergence of privately operated "commercial expeditions." These offered a guided climb up Everest that could be booked like a tour package. There was no shortage of customers, even though the price tag could run $50,000 a head. The summit of Everest now got very crowded on fine days in May. When 40 people made it to the top one afternoon in 1993, observers shook their heads glumly and predicted that this state of affairs was a recipe for disaster.

TOSSING OFFERINGS OF BARLEY FLOUR into the sky, climbers and
Sherpas of the Imax team make their *puja* at Base Camp before starting their climb.
This is a ceremony to appease the gods and beg for their protection on the mountain.
This image was shot in 1996 for the making of the Imax film, *Everest*.

"The night had a phantasmal beauty that intensified as we climbed, more stars than I had ever seen smeared the frozen sky."

—JON KRAKAUER, ON CLIMBING TO THE SUMMIT, MAY 9, 1996

Before long climbers of Hall's and Fischer's teams were strung out in one long line, along with Makalu Gau of the Taiwanese team and his Sherpas. (The South Africans had decided against setting out that day.)

During the morning, five of Hall's clients realized they could not make the summit before the cutoff time and, sensibly, they turned back—or, in the case of Beck Weathers, settled down to await the leader's return. Krakauer kept going and reached the top not long after 1 p.m., but he didn't experience the expected wave of happiness at being there. All he could think was that this was only half the climb. Several days of dangerous descent now separated him from Base Camp and safety. Meanwhile, those of us eagerly awaiting news down in Base Camp cheered as we learned over the radio of the season's first successes. Three of Rob Hall's clients got to the top, with two guides and two Sherpas, as did 13 members of Scott Fischer's team. Makalu Gau and his two Sherpas also made it. Adding in the climbers who came up from the Tibetan side, altogether 23 people stood on top of the world that day—most arriving around 2 p.m. Everyone knew that was very late in the day for retreating safely. And, waiting below, we crossed fingers anxiously.

The first hint that all was not well came at around 4 p.m. when some astonishing-looking clouds came sweeping up the Khumbu Valley. Violet-black, they roiled like burning rubber. A vicious storm was blowing in.

That evening Rob Hall radioed to say that it had taken him more than an hour to encourage his slowest client, Doug Hansen, back down the Hillary Step. They were now both out of oxygen and Hansen was unable to go farther. At that time, it would have been possible for Hall to continue alone, but he refused to leave his client, hoping that someone could bring more oxygen to them. As darkness fell, it became clear that, with the blizzard raging, very few of the returning climbers had made it back to the camp on the col. More than 20 people were strung out along the Southeast Ridge, where visibility had shrunk to a few yards.

Throughout the night, those on the col kept lights burning and banged pots to indicate where the camp was. The Kazakhi guide Anatoli Boukreev and a Canadian doctor, Stuart Hutchinson, mustered the energy to go out into the storm from time to time in search of those still missing. Four climbers struggled in around 1 a.m., telling how they'd had to leave others, who'd become disoriented, on the far, eastern, side of the col. Boukreev eventually found this group and led three exhausted members of Scott Fischer's team to safety. He could do nothing for two of Hall's clients, Beck Weathers and Yasuko Namba, who both lay inert in the snow. He thought they were probably dead, or very close to it. It was 4:30 a.m.

Nothing was heard from Rob Hall until 4:45 that morning. By now he was alone just above the South Summit. It wasn't clear what had happened to Hansen. Later, it was learned that the guide Andy Harris had climbed back to help the pair; now he too had vanished. Hall had some oxygen bottles at least, though ice blocked his breathing tube and was proving difficult to clear. He was very weak, frostbitten, and in pain. Friends at other camps did their best to encourage him by radio.

"Rob, you have to go, you have to go!" Ed Viesturs from the Imax team urged. "Turn the oxygen full on and start crawling. Crawl and pull your way up the rope."

Mount Everest
29,035 ft
8,850 m

South Summit
28,710 ft

Northeast Ridge

Southeast Ridge

South Col

Camp 4
26,000 ft

Lhotse
27,890 ft
8,501 m

North Ridge

North Face

Southwest Face

Geneva Spur

Lhotse Face

North Col

West Ridge

Camp 3
24,000 ft

Camp 2
Advance base camp
21,300 ft

Western Cwm

1996 Expeditions

—— South Col route

MOUNTAIN WITHOUT MERCY:
The South Col-Southeast Ridge route, though well-trodden in the years since its first ascent, can still be a dangerous proposition, as was demonstrated in the storm of May 10–11 1996, when five climbers died retreating from the summit to the camp on the South Col.

Several times Hall tried to stand, but he could not. Hope now hinged on being able to get Sherpas up to help him, but it was a long shot. It had taken Hall's group ten hours to cover this section on the way up. Sherpas on full oxygen might halve that time, but so much depended on the weather. Three men set out from the col at 9:35, while Viesturs kept up the encouragement.

"C'mon, c'mon," he pleaded, "once you're on the South Summit you'll start going down. You'll feel better. Rob, keep moving!"

The positions and states of other missing members was still confused. All expeditions on the south side of the mountain were united by now into a single effort of rescue and recovery. Oxygen supplies belonging to individual teams were made available for the emergency. Fit climbers from lower down moved up to help those stricken on the col, and more Sherpas were dispatched from the col to find out what had happened to Scott Fischer and Makalu Gau, 1,200 feet higher up.

Dr. Hutchinson, meanwhile, took a close look at the man and woman lying out in the snow. They were not dead, as Boukreev had supposed, but were barely breathing. No attempt was made to move them, for it didn't seem there was anything anyone could do. Some hours later, the Sherpas trying to reach Rob Hall were forced back by bad conditions, while others returned to the col with a badly frost-bitten Makalu Gau. They had been unable to assist Fischer, whom they believed to be dead.

In the middle of the afternoon something happened that was nothing short of a miracle. Beck Weathers, who had lain lifeless on the ice for 16 hours, face up to the sky, regained consciousness. He was overwhelmed with a desire to go on living—to see his family again. His face was swollen, his eyes mere slits, but though he could see nothing, he could feel a fresh wind blowing. It struck him that this must be blowing over the col, the direction in which he needed to go. He stood up and staggered into the wind.

Todd Burleson, who had arrived on the col with Peter Athans to coordinate rescue efforts, looked out from one of the tents. Someone—or something—was stumbling toward him. Arms rigidly outstretched like branches of a tree, a face blackened and crusted over, clothes half off—Burleson could not believe his eyes. He dashed out to steer the phantom into the tent, where he began administering oxygen. It was Weathers. His hands and arms were frozen solid. Burleson did not believe the man could survive.

Boukreev, too, had seen Weathers lurch into camp, "carrying his hands without gloves up in front of his body like a surrendering soldier." It confirmed in the Kazakh's mind what a slow business dying could be. If this man could survive a night exposed to the elements high on Everest, what of Fischer? He needed to be sure in his own mind that there was no hope for his friend up there. Although another blizzard was blowing in, Boukreev fought his way back up the mountain, reaching Fischer around seven o'clock. But it was too late; there was to be no second miracle. Bitterly disappointed, Boukreev said good-bye to his dead friend and retraced his steps.

That evening Rob Hall's team set up a radio/satellite phone link between the dying Hall and his wife Jan back in New Zealand. She had spoken with him earlier in the day and been kept informed of the drama. Now, though all hope was gone, they tried to boost each other's spirits.

AN ALUMINUM LADDER, made from several sections, bridges a wide crevasse in the Khumbu Icefall. Sumiyo Tsuzuki of the Imax team crosses gingerly, belayed to a fixed rope in case she falls. This image was shot in 1996 for the making of the Imax film, *Everest*.

TOO MANY, TOO HIGH, TOO LATE. Members of Scott Fischer's team descend from the Hillary Step around 4 p.m. on May 10, as the storm blows in. This photograph comes from Fischer's final roll of film.

As they said goodnight fondly, Rob assured Jan he had oxygen for the night ahead. But it was a stormy night, like the last, and all further radio calls went unanswered.

The next day, May 12, Burleson and Athans began escorting Beck Weathers down. At the Yellow Band above the Lhotse Face, Robert Schauer and Ed Viesturs of the Imax team took over the task. They were amazed at Weathers's fortitude and good humor, despite being almost blind and unable to use his hands for balance. At Camp 3 (24,000 feet) David Breashears joined them, and in close formation they continued down.

"David walked in front of me," Weathers wrote later. "I rested one arm on the back of his pack. Each time he lifted his foot off the ice, I'd slide my crampons into his print. Behind me either Ed or Robert kept a grip on my climbing harness. In this way we slowly lurched down the face."

Weathers was led into Camp 2, where Makalu Gau, the other frost-bite victim, was already receiving treatment from another expedition doctor. Both invalids were too injured to negotiate the Khumbu Icefall, so a bold helicopter airlift was organized the next day to whisk them to a hospital in Kathmandu. Climbers trampled out a landing space in the Western Cwm near Camp 1, marking it with a large red cross by dribbling Kool-Aid in the snow. Pilot Lt. Col. Madan K. C. of the Nepalese Army made two landings to pick up the invalids; it was one of the highest aerial rescues ever attempted.

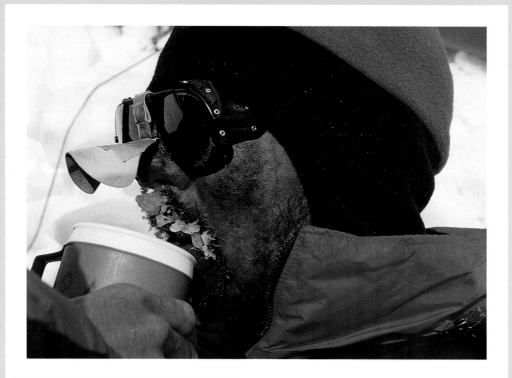

AFTER BEING LEFT FOR DEAD, Beck Weathers stood up and staggered back into camp on the South Col. After a night without shelter, he had suffered severe frostbite. Here, he is being given much needed fluids at Camp 3 on his way down the mountain.

"If this man could survive a night exposed to the elements high on Everest, what of Fischer?"

—ANATOLI BOUKREEV

At Base Camp on May 14 a memorial service was held for those lost as a result of the May 10/11 storm: the guides Scott Fischer, Rob Hall, and Andy Harris, and clients Doug Hansen and Yasuko Namba. It was also learned that three Indian climbers had perished on the north side of the mountain.

Many expeditions went home after this, but some—like the Imax team—stayed on and climbed the mountain a fortnight later. There were to be more deaths that spring. It was one of the worst seasons ever on Everest, but it has not checked the number of commercial expeditions going to the mountain each year.

Of course, the main reason this tragedy became such a big news story was that it was played out in the public eye. Before the arrival of Internet Web sites and satellite phones, one tended to hear of ordeals in remote places well after the event and when all the facts were known. The disasters of spring 1996 made it into the world's press and on television as they happened. Ordinary people became caught up in the drama, shared the the anguish of waiting for news, the frustration of being unable to help those in such peril five-and-a-half miles above the sea. And the many books written afterward, most notably by Krakauer and Boukreev, were not just read by a small band of climbers, but became international best-sellers. The actions, the errors of judgement, the disappointments, and the accusations lived on in debate for years.

Climbing Everest has become a very different kind of enterprise since Mallory and the other pioneers of the 1920s explored a way through Tibet to the summit slopes of this mighty mountain.

Conservation on Everest

Climbers and trekkers make a big impact on the fragile environment of Mount Everest and its surroundings. It has been estimated that more than 27,000 trekkers pass through the Sherpa capital of Namche Bazar each year. These visitors are welcomed and encouraged—the money they spend in the Khumbu is a lifeline for the people who live there—but that number of people can dump a lot of trash as they travel through. They take a lot of showers, drink a lot of water, and use up a lot of fuel. They abandon piles of useless plastic where no garbage trucks can cart them away and deposit a lot of bodily waste in a region that doesn't enjoy the luxury of flush toilets. No wonder the path to Everest is often called the Toilet-Paper Trail.

On Everest itself, waste has accumulated since climbing began, and very little rots away at these altitudes. Pictures show rubbish strewn at campsites on the north and south sides of Everest, and piles of discarded oxygen bottles and other items on the bleak South Col. Stories describe Everest becoming one huge pile of junk. Every so often a well-publicized clean-up expedition is organized, but at best these can only tinker with the problem. Nowadays in Nepal, the government requires every expedition to pay several thousand dollars as an environmental deposit. The money is refundable when the party goes home if—and only if—it takes out with it all its trash and toilet waste, to dispose of acceptably. At the same time, schemes exist for paying Sherpas to bring down old glass and tins and oxygen bottles from high on Everest. The idea is popular with porters, who usually only get paid for carrying supplies up. This way they get the

The accumulation of 50 years: empty oxygen bottles and other items on the bleak South Col.

chance to earn extra cash for their families. Some of the older oxygen bottles have fetched high prices as antiques and helped fund this valuable work. Even so, it is going to take quite a number of Sherpas a very long time to remove the debris of 50 years.

It's not unusual for an expedition to arrive at Everest Base Camp with a dozen or more tons of supplies and equipment. The climbers will have raised a lot of money to come here, and some may be prepared to forfeit their environmental bond to be free of the awkward and expensive task of disposing of trash and surplus gear afterward. They may face other penalties, of course, not least of which is being named and shamed by more responsible expeditioners.

There are entrepreneurial Sherpas who will come up to Base Camp and buy stores and gear left over at the end of a season. These then get resold in climbing stores in Kathmandu or in lodges along the trail—a form of recycling. Even so, whatever strategies are devised, there is no way of guaranteeing that everything brought in with an Everest expedition gets carried out again. What is really needed is a change of attitude. Triumph or failure is not the only outcome of an expedition: The impact it makes on the local landscape and way of life is equally important. Climbers and trekkers, too, need to whittle down their demands in remote places. Use imported kerosene for cooking, rather than precious local firewood. Bring less, bathe less, take trash home. That way, the pleasure of being in the mountains can be enjoyed for generations to come.

Epilogue

Fifty years of ascents have seen 15 major routes traced upon the flanks of Everest. One can't help wondering: Is that it now? Or are there yet more routes waiting to be climbed? Among themselves climbers talk of dream ventures—like the mammoth "Everest-Horseshoe." This would require climbing Everest (from the north, or by the West Ridge) and then staying high to traverse the South Col and continue around onto Lhotse and then Nuptse, before coming down. It would be an extreme undertaking, demanding superhuman fitness. Another challenge has come to be known as "Fantasy Ridge." For this, you would follow the prominent easternmost rib of the East Face—again, an excessively long route. Once the rib itself is climbed, you would still face a gruelling struggle up the bulk of the Northeast Ridge before reaching the summit. These routes are likely to stay in the imagination a long time before being realized.

Yet, for many people, a route doesn't have to be new to beckon. Everest's sheer status is enough to draw most of the Base Camp hopefuls—"Because it's there," as Mallory may or may not have said. Some climb as an escape from an increasingly harassing world. Those who find themselves repeatedly heading for the Khumbu, as does American mountaineer Pete Athans, may do so largely because they enjoy, as he says, "the camaraderie that exists between Western and Sherpa climbers and by the desire to be a part of the great common objective—the climb."

Tools and tactics have evolved almost beyond recognition since people first started coming to Everest. Even such a climber as Reinhold Messner could never have made his solo ascent without modern lightweight gear and clothing. Satellite phones and the Internet have made the high Himalaya far less remote, and the day-to-day adventure of an expedition has become public property. Hopefully the traditional code of mountaineering will endure under these new pressures: a respect for the hills, respect for fellow climbers. Such values become harder to live up to on a crowded mountain where a stranger's stupidity or misfortune can threaten the best-laid plans. Yet ambition has to be balanced with compassion and a willingness to assist others in trouble if the spirit of climbing is to be kept alive— if Everest is to remain a gleaming ideal for dreamers and climbers alike.

Cornices on the summit ridge of Everest overhang a sheer drop of 10,000 feet. Taken at 12:45 p.m. on May 29, 1953, this photo shows the first ever footprints on this ridge made by Hillary and Tenzing.

Chronology

1846–52   Surveyors working for the Great Trigonometrical Survey of India calculated that one large Himalayan peak (which they knew at first simply as "b," and later called "Peak 15") rose at least to 28,800 feet, making it probably the **highest in the world.** Within a few years calculations had been refined upward to 29,002 feet, and geographers agreed the mountain was indeed the highest above sea level.

1865   Efforts to find a universally accepted local name proved inconclusive. **Peak 15 was renamed Mount Everest** in honor of Sir George Everest, the Surveyor General who superintended much of the work of the Great Trigonometrical Survey.

1876   By this time people were discussing whether it was **humanly possible to climb such a high mountain.** American mountaineer, Miss "Meta" (Margaret Claudia) Brevoort (1825–1876), was one who gave thought to the matter, but she died before getting the chance to put her plans in motion.

1903–04   **British soldiers invaded Tibet** in an effort to forestall Russian influence, which they believed threatened the borders of British-held India. On their way to the Tibetan capital of Lhasa, they photographed Everest—that "spotless pinnacle of the world"—floating on the horizon 94 miles away. Later, it would be seen again by Captain Rawling and others, from a distance of 40 miles.

1913   **Capt. John Noel crossed secretly into Tibet,** approaching within 60 miles of Everest, before being turned back by Tibetan soldiers.

1915–16   **Plans for a British Everest expedition**, which would have included Rawling and Noel, had to be abandoned because of the First World War (1914–18). Rawling, along with many other mountaineers, was killed in the fighting. After the war, Captain Noel lectured to the Royal Geographical Society and reignited interest in scaling the great mountain.

1921   **First Everest expedition:** A British reconnaissance party under the leadership of Lt. Col. Charles Howard-Bury secured a permit to travel through Tibet to Everest. George Mallory and his old schoolchum Guy Bullock explored the northern and eastern approaches and led a small group onto the North Col. (Dr. A. K. Kellas died on the march-in.)

1922   **First climb using oxygen apparatus:** George Ingle Finch and Geoffrey Bruce, breathing supplemental oxygen, gained an altitude of 27,300 feet on the North Face of Everest. This was 215 vertical feet higher than an oxygenless attempt led by Mallory that same year.

1922   **First Everest casualties:** In one last-ditch attempt before going home, nine Sherpa porters serving this British expedition were hit by an avalanche while climbing on the slopes of the North Col. Seven died. (Sherpas have continually sustained the greatest number of fatalities on Everest.)

1924 **Col. E. F. Norton and T. Howard Somervell climbed to almost 28,000** feet without oxygen, before Somervell was forced to give up. Norton pressed on alone to 28,126 feet, until he, too, admitted defeat. Then Mallory decided to have a go, climbing with 22-year-old Andrew "Sandy" Irvine and taking oxygen apparatus. They were spotted on the summit ridge by Noel Odell, but they never returned. To this day, no one knows whether Mallory and Irvine made it to the top. (Mallory's body was found 75 years later; at the time of writing it is not certain where Irvine lies.)

1933–38 Several British expeditions failed to improve on the height gained by Norton in 1924. Meanwhile first flights over Everest provided **good aerial photographs** for detailed mapping of the summit area.

1950 **Communist China occupied Tibet**, closing it to outsiders and putting Everest out of bounds from north and east. Meanwhile a palace revolution in Nepal overthrew the ruling Rana dynasty which had kept that country in strict isolation. The first trekkers and scientists were allowed in, and a small Anglo-American party led by American Dr. Charles Houston scouted out the southern route to Everest. Following the Khumbu Glacier, they got a good look at the Khumbu Icefall and were not at all optimistic that Everest could be climbed that way.

1951 British mountaineer Eric Shipton brought in a small reconnaissance team, which included New Zealander Edmund Hillary. They managed to **scale the Khumbu Icefall** but didn't cross the large crevasse at its top.

1952 **Swiss mountaineers attempted the mountain** during the spring and fall. In May, Raymond Lambert and Tenzing Norgay reached a high point of 28,210 feet on the Southeast Ridge. It was higher than anyone had ever climbed before.

1953 **First ascent of Everest:** A British expedition led by Col. John Hunt (later Sir John Hunt, later still Lord Hunt) finally saw success by climbing the South Col/Southeast Ridge of Everest. On May 29, Ed Hillary and Tenzing Norgay stood on the snowy summit. Old-timers thought people would now lose interest in this monster mountain, allowing climbers to concentrate on other objectives. But the popularity of Everest has—like the mountain itself—kept growing.

1954 **The opening up of Nepal** had brought new possibilities for triangulating Everest from the south at much closer range than before. At the same time techniques of computation had improved. A revised height of 29,028 feet (8,848 meters) was announced.

1960 **First ascent via North Col/Northeast Ridge:** Wang Fuzhou, Gongbu and Qu Yinhua were the Sino-Tibetan summit party to claim the first ascent from the north in May. They reached the summit, they reported, in the middle of the night. It took western countries 20 years and a thaw in political relations with China to officially acknowledge the climb.

1963 **New route and first traverse:** Americans Tom Hornbein and Willi Unsoeld climbed Everest by the West Ridge and Hornbein Couloir (on the forbidden North Face). They descended by the standard Southeast Ridge and the South Col. The expedition was led by Norman Dyhrenfurth, who also made the expedition film, which included the first movie footage of the summit, taken by Lute Jerstad. President John F. Kennedy presented the National Geographic Society's coveted Hubbard Medal to members of the team.

1975   **First women on the summit:** Japanese Junko Tabei reached the summit via the South Col on May 16, with Ang Tsering Sherpa. A few days later, a second woman, Phantog of Tibet, made an ascent from the north as part of a Chinese expedition.

1975   **First ascent Southwest Face:** A post-monsoon British party, led by Chris Bonington, saw four (possibly five) of its members reach the summit using this major route, which had been tried several times before. Doug Scott and Dougal Haston summitted on September 24, Peter Boardman and Pertemba Sherpa on the 26th—the same day that Mick Burke failed to return from his summit bid.

1978   **First ascent without supplemental oxygen:** Reinhold Messner and Peter Habeler were the first to "unmask" the mountain on May 8, 1978. Neither suffered lasting ill effects.

1979   Yugoslav climbers straightened out the **West Shoulder/West Ridge route** pioneered in 1963 (i.e., starting in Nepal, they climbed the ridge without veering onto the North Face as Americans had done.)

1980   **First winter ascent:** Poles Leszek Cichy and Krzsyztof Wielicki made a February climb of the mountain. Later the same year Jerzy Kukuczka and Andrzej Czok reached the summit via the South Pillar to the right of the Southwest Face. Leader in both cases was Andrzej Zawada.

1980   **First full North Face ascent:** Japanese mountaineers Tsuneoh Shigehiro and Ozaki Takashi completed first full ascent of Everest's North Face on May 10.

1980   **First solo ascent:** Reinhold Messner reached the summit on August 20, having climbed the North Col and North Face completely alone, and without using extra oxygen. This was also the first ascent made during the monsoon period.

1982   Russian climbers forged a **new route on the Southwest Face,** known as the Southwest Pillar. Eleven Soviet climbers reached the summit this way between May 4 and 9.

1983   **First East Face ascent:** American climbers establish a new route on the awesome East, or Kangshung, Face of Everest. Summit was reached on October 8 by Lou Reichardt, Kim Momb, and Carlos Buhler, and one day later by George Lowe, Jay Cassell, and Dan Reid.

1984   Another impressive line called "White Limbo" was traced on the **North Face** in October by Tim Macartney-Snape and Greg Mortimer of a four-man Australian team. They climbed without oxygen.

1986   Sharon Wood from Canada became the **first North American woman to climb Everest** when she summitted with Dwayne Congdon on May 20, having climbed the West Ridge/Hornbein Couloir from the Tibetan side.

1988   **A new line was made on the Kangshung Face** by a lightweight Anglo-American party (to the left of the 1983 route, joining the Southeast Ridge at the South Col). Stephen Venables summitted alone on May 12.

1995 **First full ascent Northeast Ridge:** Climbing from the East Rongbuk Glacier, two Japanese and four Sherpas (Kiyoshi Furuno, Shigeki Imoto, Dawa Tshering II, Pasang Kami, Khakpa Nuru, Nima Dorje) reached the summit on May 11. (All sections of this extremely long route had been climbed previously, including the difficult pinnacled section leading up to the Northeast Shoulder; but they had not been linked.)

1996 **First ascent of Zakharov's Couloir:** Russian mountaineers identified and climbed a new North Face route (North-Northeast Couloir) that gains the Northeast Ridge from the head of the East Rongbuk Glacier while avoiding the North Col and North Ridge. Danger from stonefall in this steep couloir was considerable. The summit was reached by Peter Kuznetzov, Valeri Kohanov, and Grigori Semikolenkov on May 20.

1996 A record number of **15 people died** climbing Mount Everest during this year, 8 of them in or as a result of a bad storm on May 10–11.

1999 **George Mallory's body was discovered** just below 27,000 feet by Conrad Anker, member of an expedition led by Eric Simonson and devoted to searching for clues to what happened on Mallory's 1924 expedition. It was clear from the body's position that Mallory had suffered a fall, and, from the broken rope around his waist, that his partner, Sandy Irvine, must have been with him at the time. Artifacts found on and with the body told a lot about high-altitude mountaineering 75 years before, but gave no conclusive proof of how high Mallory and Irvine had climbed.

1999 Having successfully installed and operated GPS (Global Positioning System) satellite equipment at the very top of Everest, yet another **"New Official Height for Everest" was announced** on November 11 by the National Geographic Society and Boston Museum of Science. Bradford Washburn, who had instigated much of the work using this new technology, told mountaineers that Everest was seven feet higher than had been thought. The revised altitude—29,035 feet (8,850 meters)—would begin appearing on maps. It referred to the highest bedrock and not to the snow cover, which was variable; and readings had indicated that the horizontal position of Everest was moving steadily and slightly north-eastward by about 2.4 inches a year.

2000 Babu Chhiri Sherpa climbed from the Nepalese Base Camp to the summit of Everest in **16 hours, 56 minutes**.

2001 At the age of 16 and a few weeks, Temba Tsheri Sherpa became the **youngest person to summit Mount Everest** (climbing the northern side); while in the same season on a different expedition American Sherman Bull, at 64, became the oldest.

2002 On May 16, a record 54 people reached the summit of Mount Everest, including Tashi Wangchuk Tenzing, grandson of Tenzing Norgay, and Yves Lambert, son of Raymond Lambert who, with Tenzing, almost reached the top 50 years earlier. Appa (Apa) Sherpa made his 12th Everest ascent, declaring it would be his last. The record was smashed a few days later on May 23 when an amazing 89 people made it to the top.

Everest Hall of Fame

Note: *dates are listed where information is available.*

CONRAD ANKER (b. 1964) American climber who discovered George Mallory's body on Everest in 1999. Later he free-climbed the "Second Step," high on Everest's Northeast Ridge to ascertain whether Mallory could have surmounted this difficult cliff in 1924 without assistance.

PETER ATHANS (b. 1957) has led more than a dozen Everest expeditions, attempting five different routes. He has been to the summit seven times, more than any other Western mountaineer.

APPA or APA (b. 1961?) The Sherpa who currently holds the record for the most repeat ascents of Everest. In 2002, at the age of 41, he paid his 12th visit to the roof of the world, then announced his retirement from Everest-climbing.

BABU CHHIRI SHERPA (1966–2000) Another modern-day Sherpa mountaineer who set a number of Everest records, including the fastest ascent—under 17 hours. That was in 2000; in the previous year he spent 21 hours on the summit itself. Babu, who was 35, died when he fell into an Everest crevasse in 2001.

BARRY BISHOP (1932–1994) Mountain geographer and photographer, who climbed Everest with the 1963 American expedition. Forced to bivouac in the open at 28,000 feet, he lost all his toes and parts of his fingers to frostbite. Bishop worked on the staff of the National Geographic Society for 35 years.

BRENT BISHOP (b. 1966) Son of Barry Bishop, Brent made the first of his several Everest ascents in 1994. He is committed to cleaning up Everest so that it may be enjoyed for generations to come.

SIR CHRIS BONINGTON (b. 1934) British mountaineer, born in 1934, has led several Everest expeditions, including the first successful climb of the Southwest Face in 1975.

ANATOLI BOUKREEV (1958–1997) This strong Russian mountaineer, who climbed Everest four times in all, saved the lives of several climbers in the great storm of May 1996 when he was head guide to Scott Fischer's expedition. He died the following year on Annapurna, another major Himalayan peak.

TOM BOURDILLON (1924–1956) took part in the 1951 reconnaissance of the south side of Everest. With Charles Evans in 1953 he became the first to reach Everest's South Summit, using closed-circuit oxygen apparatus that he'd designed with his scientist father.

DAVID BREASHEARS (b. 1955) This climber-filmmaker has made several Everest films, including the celebrated Imax *Everest,* shot in 1996. His first live broadcast from the summit in 1983 earned him

an Emmy Award, as did the film he shot with Kurt Diemberger of the East Face in 1981.

GENERAL CHARLES BRUCE (1866–1939) Distinguished soldier of the Northwest Frontier of India, whose wheezing laugh was said to be a tonic the length and breadth of the Himalaya. He led the expedition of 1922, but was forced to withdraw from the leadership in 1924 by a bad bout of malaria.

GEOFFREY BRUCE (1896–1972) A soldier cousin of General Bruce, put in charge of transport arrangements for the expedition of 1922. Not a trained mountaineer, his first serious climb was a summit attempt that year with Finch, when the pair used oxygen for the first time ever on Everest to reach a record 27,300 feet. In 1924 he was a full climbing member of the team.

GEORGE INGLE FINCH (1888–1970) A scientist by profession, Finch was the first to demonstrate the usefulness of oxygen apparatus on Everest. With it in 1922, he and Geoffrey Bruce climbed to 27,300 feet, a new record. He was also the first to use eiderdown clothing for insulation against the mountain's cold.

SCOTT FISCHER (1956–1996) From Seattle, this charismatic mountaineer and tour leader was one of eight who perished high on Everest in the fierce storm of May 10–11, 1996.

GONGBU A Tibetan mountaineer who reached the summit of Everest in 1960 with a Chinese expedition and went on to have a long career in mountaineering management with the Tibet Mountaineering Association. He is now retired.

PETER HABELER (b. 1942) Austrian mountain and ski guide who, with Reinhold Messner in 1978, climbed Everest for the first time without breathing extra oxygen.

ROB HALL (1961–1996) Experienced high-altitude mountaineer and tour organizer, who climbed Everest five times. He died near the South Summit of Everest in May 1996, having lingered to assist an ailing tour member, who also perished. Hall was in radio contact with lower camps and—when close to death—was patched in to speak with his wife back home in New Zealand.

ALISON HARGREAVES (1962–1995) British mountaineer, who in 1995 made a solo ascent of Everest from the north side. Though others were on the mountain at the same time, Hargreaves accepted no assistance from anyone, not even a cup of tea, and she climbed without oxygen apparatus. Later that same year she was killed attempting K2 (the world's second highest mountain.)

DOUGAL HASTON (1940–1977) Scottish mountaineer. With Doug Scott, Haston was first to complete the climb of Everest's Southwest Face in

1975, surviving a night out on the South Summit on the way down.

SIR EDMUND HILLARY (b. 1919) First ever—with Tenzing Norgay on May 29, 1953—to trample Mount Everest's summit snows. Born in New Zealand, young Ed Hillary grew up to be a beekeeper. After Everest he devoted his life and celebrity to the welfare of the Sherpa people of Nepal, building schools and hospitals in their mountain home.

DR. TOM HORNBEIN (b. 1930) This anesthesiologist made a new route up Everest's West Ridge and completed the first traverse of Everest in 1963 with philosopher-climber, Willi Unsoeld. Hornbein's best-selling book *Everest: The West Ridge* has been continuously in print ever since.

CHARLES K. HOWARD-BURY (1883–1963) In 1920 Lieutenant Colonel Howard-Bury spent four months in India and Tibet negotiating permission for the first Everest expedition, which he led the following year on behalf of the British Alpine Club and Royal Geographical Society.

LORD HUNT (1910–1998) Career soldier, diplomat, and parliamentarian, John Hunt was chosen to lead the British Mount Everest expedition of 1953, and his superior planning and organization contributed enormously to its successful first ascent of the mountain.

ANDREW (SANDY) IRVINE (1902–1924) This Oxford University student was the youngest member on the 1924 British expedition. Just 22 years old, he lost his life going for the summit with his partner George Mallory.

GÖRAN KROPP (1966–2002) A modern-day Viking adventurer, Kropp cycled to Nepal from his home in Sweden, ferried his own equipment to the mountain, and climbed Everest in 1996 without oxygen, before setting out to cycle home again. Three years later he came again to escort his girlfriend to the top.

GEORGE LEIGH MALLORY (1886–1924) The schoolmaster who went to Everest three times in the 1920s "because it's there!" He was lost with Andrew Irvine climbing for the summit in 1924, and his body was not found for 75 years. No one knows whether he and Irvine reached the summit before they died.

REINHOLD MESSNER (b. 1944) This South Tyrolean climber climbed Everest from Nepal in 1978 with Peter Habeler, making the first-ever ascent without the aid of supplementary oxygen. Two years later, completely on his own, he climbed a new route on the Tibetan side of the mountain, again without using oxygen.

NAWANG GOMBU (b. 1936) This Sherpa nephew of Tenzing Norgay was the first man to climb Everest twice, in 1963 with American mountaineers, and two years later with an Indian expedition.

CAPT. JOHN NOEL (1890–1989) This soldier-explorer became the first filmmaker of Everest. In 1922 and 1924 he shot silent film of the earliest climbing attempts. He died in 1989, shortly after his 99th birthday.

PROFESSOR NOEL ODELL (1890–1987) A geologist, Odell was examining the rocks high on Everest when, in June 1924, he caught the last glimpse of Mallory and Irvine making their tragic bid for the summit. Twice he climbed alone to 27,500 feet in search of the two men, who failed to return.

PHANTOG Tibetan woman, married to a Chinese climber. She reached the summit from the north with the Chinese expedition of 1975.

QU YINHUA Chinese forestry worker who in 1960 made the first authenticated ascent of Mallory's Northeast Ridge climb with fellow climbers Wang Fu Zhou and Gongbu. Qu found a way up the Second Step but suffered severe frostbite in the process.

ERIC SHIPTON (1907–1977) Famous explorer and one of the most gifted climbers of his generation, Shipton took part in all four official Everest expeditions of the 1930s. In 1951, he led the reconnaissance of the mountain's southern slopes, scouting a way through the notorious Khumbu Icefall.

TENZING NORGAY (1914–1986) As a child, Tenzing herded yaks below Everest, and he grew up to be one of the first pair to climb the great mountain, bringing fame to the Sherpa people of Nepal. He lived in Darjeeling, India, where he helped found the Himalayan Mountaineering Institute "to train a thousand Tenzings." He died there in 1986 at age 72.

DOUG SCOTT (b. 1941) British mountaineer who climbed the Southwest Face of Everest with Dougal Haston in 1975. They survived an open bivouac without frostbite.

JUNKO TABEI (b. 1941) This Japanese housewife and businesswoman made the first female ascent of Everest in 1975. It was the 39th ascent overall.

WILLI UNSOELD (1926–1979) This charismatic climber and teacher from Oregon made the first traverse of Everest with Tom Hornbein in 1963.

WANG FUZHOU Trained as a geologist, Wang was one of the first three to complete the northern route to the summit on the Chinese expedition of 1960. He went on to work for the Chinese Mountaineering Association, making many friends around the world.

KRZYSZTOF WIELICKI (b. 1950) With Leszech Cichy made the first winter ascent of Everest on February 17, 1980. Wielicki, from Poland, went on to climb all 14 of the highest mountains in the world.

MAURICE WILSON (1898–1934) An eccentric ex-soldier who in 1934 believed that with praying and fasting, he could climb Mount Everest alone. He piloted himself from England to India in a light airplane, then traveled in disguise through Tibet to Everest. But the North Col defeated him, and he perished in his tent at Advance Base Camp, where his body and diary were found the following year.

The Record Breakers

FIRST TO CLIMB MOUNT EVEREST
Edmund Hillary and Tenzing Norgay on May 29, 1953, in the course of the ninth official British expedition to Everest, led by Colonel Hunt. They climbed via the South Col and Southeast Ridge.

FIRST AMERICAN ON THE SUMMIT
James Whittaker on May 1, 1963.

FIRST WOMEN ON THE SUMMIT
Japanese Junko Tabei reached the summit via the South Col on May 16, 1975; a few days later Phantog from Tibet made the ascent from the north.

FIRST TO CLIMB EVEREST WITHOUT BOTTLED OXYGEN
Reinhold Messner and Peter Habeler in the spring of 1978.

FIRST WINTER ASCENT
Polish mountaineers Leszek Cichy and Krzysztof Wielicki in February 1980.

FIRST SOLO ASCENT
Reinhold Messner soloed Everest over three days during the monsoon season in August 1980. He used no bottled oxygen.

FIRST MARRIED COUPLE
Andrej and Marija Stremfelj of Slovenia stepped on to the summit together in October 1990.

FATHER AND SON
Alpine guide Jean Roche and his 17-year-old son Bertrand summitted together in October 1990. They then descended from the South Col using a two-man paraglider.

FIRST FRATERNAL ASCENT
Spanish brothers Alberto and Felix Inurrategui climbed Everest in September 1992.

FIRST ASCENT BY AMPUTEE
Naturalized American climber Tom Whittaker, who lost his right foot in a car accident, became the first amputee to climb Everest in 1998.

LONGEST TIME ON TOP
One of Babu Chhiri Sherpa's many records was to spend 21 hours on the summit of Everest in a small tent in 2000.

SPEEDIEST ASCENTS
In May 1996 a superbly acclimatized Hans Kammerlander climbed the north side of Everest from Advance Base Camp in 16 hours, 45 minutes. Skiing back down, he made the round trip in less than 24 hours. On the southern side in May 2000 Babu Chhiri Sherpa raced to the summit from the Khumbu Base Camp via the South Col in only 16 hours, 56 minutes.

CYCLIST
Göran Kropp bicycled from Sweden to climb Everest, reached the summit in lightweight fashion in May 1996, and cycled most of the way back home again.

SKI RECORD
In October 2000 Davo Karnicar skied nonstop down the south side of Everest in less than five hours.

SPEEDIEST DESCENT
Bertrand Roche and his wife, Claire Bernier, climbed Everest from the north then flew from the summit on a tandem paraglider, to land at Advance Base Camp 8 minutes later.

FIRST BLIND EVERESTER
In 2001 American Erik Weihenmayer became the first blind person to summit.

OLDEST EVEREST CLIMBER
American Sherman Bull reached the summit in 2001 at age 64.

YOUNGEST EVEREST CLIMBER
Temba Tsheri Sherpa, age 16, summitted from the north side on May 24, 2001.

EVEREST SNOWBOARDER
Marco Siffredi (France) completed a snowboard descent of the North Face in two and a half hours on May 23, 2001.

Resource Guide

BOOKS

Band, George.
Everest (The Official 50th Anniversary Volume). London: Harper Collins, 2003.

Boukreev, Anatoli, and G. Weston DeWalt.
The Climb. New York: St. Martins Press, 1997, 1999.

Breashears, David, and Audrey Salkeld.
Last Climb: The Legendary Everest Expeditions of George Mallory. Washington, D.C.: National Geographic Society, 1999.

Coburn, Broughton.
Everest: Mountain without Mercy. Washington: National Geographic Society, 1997, and paperback reprint 2002.

Coburn, Broughton.
Triumph on Everest: A Photobiography of Sir Edmund Hillary. Washington, D.C.: National Geographic Society, 2000.

Douglas, Ed.
Tenzing: Hero of Everest. Washington, D.C.: National Geographic Society, 2003.

Gillman, Peter (Editor).
Everest, Eighty Years of Triumph and Tragedy. Boston/New York/London: Little Brown, 2001 (new edition.)

Gillman, Peter, and Leni Gillman.
The Wildest Dream: Mallory, His Life and Conflicting Passions. London: Headline, 2000.

Hemmleb, Jochen, with Larry A. Johnson and Eric Simonson.
Ghosts of Everest: The Search for Mallory and Irvine. Seattle: The Mountaineers/London: Macmillan, 1999.

Hemmleb, Jochen, and Eric Simonson.
Detectives on Everest: The 2001 Mallory and Irvine Research Expedition. Seattle: The Mountaineers, 2002.

Holzel, Tom, and Audrey Salkeld. *The Mystery of Mallory and Irvine.* London: Cape, 1986; Revised Seattle: The Mountaineers, 1999.

Hunt, Sir John.
The Ascent of Everest. London: Hodder & Stoughton, 1953/New York: Dutton, 1954, and regularly reprinted.

Kielkowski, Jan.
Mount Everest Massif monograph, guide, chronicle. Gliwice (Poland): Explo 1993, Revised and enlarged, 2000.

Krakauer, Jon.
Into Thin Air. New York: Villard/London: Macmillan, 1997, and many reprints.

Messner, Reinhold.
Everest, Expedition to the Ultimate. London: Bâton Wicks/Seattle: The Mountaineers (new edition), 1999.

Messner, Reinhold.
The Crystal Horizon. Everest— The First Solo Ascent. Marlborough: Crowood/Seattle: The Mountaineers (new edition), 1998.

Salkeld, Audrey.
Mystery on Everest: A Photobiography of George Mallory. Washington, D.C.: National Geographic Society, 2000.

Salkeld, Audrey and John Boyle.
Climbing Mount Everest: The biography (The literature and history of climbing the world's highest mountain.) Lazonby: Sixways Publishing (revised edition) 2003.

Summers, Julie.
Fearless on Everest: The Quest for Sandy Irvine. London: Weidenfeld & Nicolson, 2000, and reprinted.

Unsworth, Walt.
Everest. Seattle: The Mountaineers/London: Bâton Wicks (revised edition), 1999.

Zhou Zheng and Liu Zhenkai.
Footprints on the Peaks: Mountaineering in China. Seattle: Cloudcap, 1995.

MAGAZINE ARTICLES

Anker, Conrad.
"Mystery on Everest." NATIONAL GEOGRAPHIC, October 1999.

Harvard, Andrew.
"The Forgotten Face of Everest." NATIONAL GEOGRAPHIC, July 1984.

Messner, Reinhold
"At My Limit—I Climbed Mount Everest Alone." NATIONAL GEOGRAPHIC, October 1981.

Roberts, David.
"Out of Thin Air." *National Geographic Adventure,* Fall 1999.

special Everest editions of *National Geographic Kids,* May 2003, NATIONAL GEOGRAPHIC, May 2003 and *National Geographic Adventure,* April 2003.

MAP

National Geographic map products:
Mount Everest/Himalaya topographic wall map
Adventure Maps of Nepal (trekking maps)
To order: 800-962-1643 or www.nationalgeographic.com/maps

VIDEOS

The Mystery of Mallory and Irvine. 1986 film, available from Nova, Public Broadcasting Service, 1999.

Lost on Everest. Nova, Public Broadcasting Service, 2000.

Lost on Everest. BBC, London, 1999.

National Geographic Everest video and DVD coming Spring 2003

WEB SITES TO VISIT
www.adventurestats.com
www.everesthistory.com
www.everestnews.com
www.mounteverest.net
www.news.nationalgeographic.com
www.pbs.org/wgbh/nova/everest

Glossary

abseil Climber's method of descending steep ground by a controlled slide down a rope.

acclimatization Gradual process whereby the body adapts (to an extent) to functioning at the lower air pressures found at high altitudes. At 16,000 feet the amount of oxygen available is half that at sea level; above 26,000 feet it's only a third.

alpinism Mountaineering that involves climbing on snow, ice and rock—as would be encountered in the Alps (or other snowy ranges.) A climber practicing this may be called an alpinist.

altitude sickness Discomfort brought about by climbing to unaccustomed heights, where the air is thinner than at sea level, particularly if you have made the transition too quickly. Headaches, nausea and breathlessness are the main symptoms, and they shouldn't be ignored. Don't go higher while the symptoms persist. Let the body acclimatize first.

belaying This is a way of protecting climbers when they are climbing together on a rope. Only one person moves at a time, the other (or it could be others) remaining firmly tied to the mountain. This is done either by tying directly onto a rock feature, or by using pegs, rope-slings or other climbing equipment to attach yourself. With good belays, if a leader falls, he (or she) cannot pull off any other member of the party. And if the second has been managing the rope efficiently, paying out only what the leader needs at the time, then the leader's fall will be limited to the length of the paid-out rope. Solo climbers have developed ways of belaying themselves to safeguard dangerous moves.

bivouac Temporary overnight stop without a tent. Lightweight wind- or waterproof "bivvy bags" are a sensible precaution if you are likely to be caught out. At high altitudes climbers may try to dig a snowhole to bivouac in, or huddle down between rocks. At very high altitudes, it is unwise to sleep. You should keep rubbing and slapping yourself and your partner to maintain circulation.

col A pass or dip in a ridge between two peaks, usually offering the easiest passage from one side to the other. Also called a "saddle."

cornice An unsupported mass of wind-sculpted snow or ice overhanging the crest of a ridge.

couloir A gully or trench running down a mountain face. While a couloir may offer an obvious way up a slope, it also provides a channel down which stones and avalanches can travel, so needs approaching with care.

crampons The framed metal spikes a climber straps to the soles of his or her boots for moving on snow and ice. Usually has 10 or 12 points to each foot. If 12, the front pair point forward for steep ice work.

crevasse A split in a glacier's surface, caused as the ice stream moves over bumps in the glacier bed, or the flow is constricted, or if it widens out. Some crevasses can be very deep, and all are dangerous when concealed by new snow.

cwm This is a Welsh word for a deep, steep-sided hollow carved by ice. The Western Cwm on Everest was named by George Mallory, who was familiar with lesser cwms in North Wales.

Dalai Lama This is the name of the spiritual head of Tibetan buddhism. In the early years of Everest exploration when Tibet was independent, the Dalai Lama was also the head of state.

frostbite Damage, or gangrene, which can occur in extreme cold as the body's circulation cuts back to protect inner organs. It affects the extremities first: fingers, toes, ears, nose. In bad cases the damage is permanent and the tissues die, necessitating surgical removal. Very bad cases can be fatal.

glacier A river of ice that moves slowly down a valley from above the snowline.

GPS (Global Positioning System) A satellite navigation system. A small handheld receiver picks up satellite signals and displays coordinates on its screen. It tells you within a small margin of error where you are on Earth's surface. The system also has important scientific uses for mapmaking, etc.

HACE, HAPE These are life-threatening medical conditions, brought on by climbing too high or too quickly (see page 80). The only effective treatment is to lose altitude fast.

icefall A steep, broken section of a glacier where it flows over a sizeable drop in its bed. It is always unstable and has to be approached with caution. Many of the deaths on Everest, especially in the old days, occurred on the icefall slopes of the North Col or in the Khumbu Icefall.

karabiner A snap link, often oval or D-shaped, used for attaching to ropes: climber to rope, rope to belay; or as a runner for abseiling. Sometimes spelled "carabiner."

lee Out of the wind; the shelter given by neighboring rock or other feature.

monsoon A seasonal wind and weather system. In the Himalaya of Nepal and Tibet it brings rain, snow, and storms during the period from June to August.

moraine Rock debris piled up by the movement of glaciers or ice sheets. Moraine heaps are found particularly at the sides and the end of a glacier (or where a glacier used to be).

pass A passable gap through a mountain barrier, usually the easiest or lowest way through. It could be a col.

piton A metal peg hammered into a crack to support a belay. You can buy them in a variety of shapes for different size cracks and the different jobs you want them to do. Sometimes called "pegs," "pins," or "nails." Pegs for belaying on ice are usually fashioned as a screw.

primus stove A portable camping cooker burning vaporized kerosene (paraffin) or gasoline.

scree Broken rock debris at the foot of a cliff.

sérac A tower or pinnacle of ice, found especially in icefalls or peeling off of ice cliffs. Usually dangerously unstable.

Sherpas An ethnic group of Tibetan origin, living in the Khumbu region of Nepal, below Everest. The word is often applied to all Nepalese who work as high-altitude porters, though these days these can be Tamangs, Rai, etc., as well as true Sherpas.

sirdar The head Sherpa of an expedition, who works directly with the leader.

spindrift Loose powder snow blown by wind or avalanche blast.

tectonic plates The Earth's surface is composed of a series of rigid plates that slide around over geological time, changing relationship with one another. Plate tectonics is the study of this movement.

windslab A type of avalanche that can occur when hard, wind-compacted snow sits insecurely on softer old snow. When triggered by movement, it tends to break up into enormous blocks or slabs.

yak A large, big-horned, hairy, humped ox, specially adapted to life at high altitudes. Yaks have been domesticated as beasts of burden by Tibetans and Sherpas, but they remain unpredictable in temperament. Often they are crossbred with more docile types of cattle.

Credits

Index

Photographs are indicated by **boldface.** If photographs are included within a page span, the entire span is boldface.

You are a child of the universe,
No less than the trees and stars;
You have a right to be here.
And whether or not it is clear to you,
No doubt the universe is unfolding as it should.

—Max Ehrmann

BELOVED DEVIN
OCTOBER 27, 1964 - MARCH 17, 2000

The Devin Shafron Memorial Book Fund